THE 2012 RHYSLING ANTHOLOGY

Also available from the
Science Fiction Poetry Association

The Alchemy of Stars: Rhysling Award Winners Showcase
Edited by Roger Dutcher and Mike Allen

The Science Fiction Poetry Handbook
Suzette Haden Elgin

The 2011 Rhysling Anthology: The Best Science Fiction, Fantasy, and Horror Poetry of 2010
Edited by David Lunde

The 2010 Rhysling Anthology: The Best Science Fiction, Fantasy, and Horror Poetry of 2009
Edited by Jaime Lee Moyer

The 2009 Rhysling Anthology: The Best SF, Fantasy, and Horror Poetry of 2008
Edited by Drew Morse

The 2008 Rhysling Anthology: The Best SF, Fantasy, and Horror Poetry of 2007
Edited by Drew Morse

THE 2012 RHYSLING ANTHOLOGY

THE BEST SCIENCE FICTION,
FANTASY, AND HORROR
POETRY OF 2011

SELECTED BY THE
SCIENCE FICTION
POETRY ASSOCIATION

EDITED BY
Lyn C. A. Gardner

Copyright © 2012
by the Science Fiction Poetry Association
in the names of the individual contributors.
All works used by permission.

All subsidiary rights to individual works herein belong to the author or current copyright holder. All rights pertaining to the publication itself are reserved. No part of this body of text as presented may be reproduced by any process in present, past, or future use without permission of the Science Fiction Poetry Association (via its current head officer at the time of request) and pertinent copyright holders, except in the case of brief quotations embodied in critical or analytical reviews or articles.

Editor and Rhysling chair: Lyn C. A. Gardner
Layout and design: Robert Frazier
Cover design: David Lee Summers
Publisher: Science Fiction Poetry Association
Published in cooperation with: Hadrosaur Productions
SFPA president: David C. Kopaska-Merkel

About the cover: Image by T. A. Rector/University of Alaska Anchorage, H. Schweiker/WIYN and National Optical Astronomy Observatory/Association of Universities for Research in Astronomy/National Science Foundation. This image was obtained with the wide-field view of the Mosaic Camera on the Mayall 4-meter telescope at Kitt Peak National Observatory. This globule is located just south of vdB 141, a reflection nebula located in the constellation Cepheus. This very faint nebula looks like a bird about to take flight. North is down and east is to the right. Imaged August 28, 2009.

Cataloging-in-Publication Data

The 2012 Rhysling anthology : the best science fiction, fantasy, and horror poetry of 2011 / selected by the Science Fiction Poetry Association ; edited by Lyn C. A. Gardner.
    p. cm.
    Includes bibliographical references.
    ISBN 978-1-885093-63-9
    1. Poetry. 2. Science fiction poetry. 3. Fantasy poetry. 4. Horror poetry.
    I. Gardner, Lyn C. A., 1970-
811'.0080'30876—dc23

For more information on the
Science Fiction Poetry Association,
visit **www.sfpoetry.com**

CONTENTS

- 8 **Preface:** Lyn C. A. Gardner
- 10 **The Rhysling Awards:** A Brief Introduction
- 11 **Acknowledgments**
- 14 **2012 Voting Procedures**

Short Poems First Published in 2011
- 15 Mary Alexandra Agner, "Venus to Her Terraformers"
- 15 Camille Alexa, "Young Miss Frankenstein Regrets"
- 16 Erik Amundsen, "The Lend"
- 17 Elizabeth Barrette, "The Shipwright's Song"
- 17 Robert Borski, "Abel"
- 19 Bruce Boston, "The Music of Robots"
- 19 Rich Boucher, "Response to Botticelli"
- 20 G. O. Clark, "Peter and Alice"
- 21 P. S. Cottier, "Fingernails"
- 21 Becca De La Rosa, "World's End"
- 22 James S. Dorr, "Monkey See"
- 23 Denise Dumars, "Folding Money"
- 23 Martin Elster, "My Unicorn"
- 24 Timons Esaias, "Dark Matter"
- 25 Kendall Evans, "Dragon"
- 26 Angel Favazza, "Clothes of Yesterday"
- 26 Janis Freegard, "Yayoi Kusama goes to Iceland"
- 27 Lyn C. A. Gardner, "In Translation"
- 27 T. M. Göttl, "Bridges"
- 28 Neile Graham, "The Bean-Sidhe Calls in Owl-Light"
- 29 Neile Graham, "The Ones Outside Your Door"
- 30 John Grey, "Mr. and Mrs. Goodnight"
- 31 Sandra Kasturi, "Ode to the Mongolian Death Worm"
- 32 Roz Kaveney, "Fembot"
- 32 Keith Kennedy, "First Loves for the First Time"
- 33 Nicole Kornher-Stace, "The Witch's Heart"
- 34 B. J. Lee, "The Tortoise's Encounter"
- 35 Greg Leunig, "Love in the Quantum Era"
- 36 Shira Lipkin, "The Library, After"
- 37 C. S. MacCath, "When I Arrived, This Is What She Said."
- 37 Elizabeth R. McClellan, "Down Cycles"
- 38 Dawn McDuffie, "Thank God for Proust"
- 39 Joanne Merriam, "Love in the Time of Alien Invasion"
- 39 Kurt Newton, "Nuclear Stockpile Janitor"
- 39 Scott Nickell, "Response to Poe's 'Sonnet—To Science'"
- 40 Juan Manuel Perez, "Vanity"

41 Tim Pratt, "Lion Heart"
42 Sofía Rhei, translated by Lawrence Schimel, "The Magic Walnut"
42 Matthew Richards, "Ravel: An Etymology"
43 Andrew Rihn, "The Physics Major Agrees to Take the English Major Stargazing"
44 Ty Russell, "The Seas of Time"
44 R. Paul Sardanas and Tisha Garcia, "Luna Satyricon"
45 Ann K. Schwader, "the more space"
45 Ann K. Schwader, "Past Human"
46 Alexandra Seidel, "Lanterns"
47 John W. Sexton, "slit sea cucumber"
47 Marge Simon, "The Human Guest"
48 Marge Simon, "Visitors"
48 Robin Spriggs, "The Elusive Language of Purple Birds"
49 Heidy Steidlmayer, "Grendel's Mother"
49 W. Gregory Stewart, "idiointerventionist (or, 'but I interrupt myself')"
50 Anna Sykora, "Dead Hotels"
51 Sonya Taaffe, "Taking the Auspices"
51 James E. Tolan, "Red Grown"
52 Mary Turzillo, "Graffiti Tree"
52 Mary Turzillo, "Moving to Enceladus"
53 Anna Waite, "To the ancients, the sea was a dangerous place"
54 Kyla Lee Ward, "The Kite"
55 Gerald Warfield, "A Greater Moon"
56 Jacqueline West, "Escaping the Dawn"
56 Neal Wilgus, "A Modest Suggestion"
57 Stephen M. Wilson, "Angel's Den"
57 Stephen M. Wilson, "Christogenesis"
58 Greer Woodward, "Closure"

Long Poems First Published in 2011
59 Mike Allen, Sonya Taaffe, and Nicole Kornher-Stace, "The King of Cats, the Queen of Wolves"
63 Erik Amundsen, "Desfixion"
67 Megan Arkenberg, "The Curator Speaks in the Department of Dead Languages"
68 Elizabeth Barrette, "The Cathedral of the Michaelangelines"
71 Dana Bell, "Welcomed Cast Outs"
73 Robert Borski, "Gavage"
74 Bruce Boston, "Surreal Fortune"
77 g. sutton breiding, "Letter from the Golden Age"
78 Benjamin Cartwright, "Terraforming Mars"
80 G. O. Clark and Kendall Evans, "The 25-Cent Rocket: One-Quarter of the Way to the Stars"
82 C. S. E. Cooney, "Postcards from Mars"
83 Lyn C. A. Gardner, "The Chant of the Black Cats"
85 Lyn C. A. Gardner, "The Witch Girl"
86 Albert Goldbarth, "Summary: Kinetic vs. Potential"

88	April Grant, "Wallpaper"
90	Sally Rosen Kindred, "Wendy Darling Has Bad Dreams"
91	Rose Lemberg, "In the Third Cycle"
96	Shira Lipkin, "The Changeling's Lament"
98	Elissa Malcohn, "The Last Dragon Slayer"
101	Helen Marshall, "Beautiful Monster"
102	Helen Marshall, *Skeleton Leaves: A Collection*
116	Elizabeth R. McClellan, "The Walking Man Goes Looking for the Sons of John: Six Cantos"
120	Joanne Merriam, "Tender Aliens"
122	Mari Ness, "Snowmelt"
125	Paul Park, "Ragnarok"
133	Sofia Samatar, "Girl Hours"
135	Alexandra Seidel, "A Masquerade in Four Voices"
136	Nancy Sheng, "Guan Yin in the Garden"
138	Michael Shorb, "Ahura Mazda"
141	J. E. Stanley, "Speaking to the Hangman Is Not Permitted"
143	Mary Turzillo, "The Legend of the Emperor's Space Suit (A Tale of Consensus Reality)"
148	Catherynne M. Valente, "The Melancholy of Mechagirl"
151	Catherynne M. Valente, "The Secret of Being a Cowboy"
154	JoSelle Vanderhooft, "Blood, Snow, Birch and Underworld"
159	Caitlin Meredith Walsh, "Initiation"
161	Kyla Lee Ward, "The Soldier's Return"
163	Shannon Connor Winward, "All Souls' Day"
164	Greer Woodward, "Ribbons of the Sun"
166	Xanadu (Ofnguyenfame), "Mood of Mind (I)—*Tu Bi Hi Xa*"
168	**The Rhysling Award Winners 1978-2012**
171	**How to Join the SFPA**

PREFACE

GOODBYE AND HELLO, AS ALWAYS

I came in at the Rhyslings.

Long before I knew there was a Rhysling Award, I loved Robert A. Heinlein's "The Green Hills of Earth," which I first encountered on cassette at my local library, read by Leonard Nimoy (with a hilarious flip side, "Gentlemen, Be Seated"). Finding such science fiction gems at the library helped me while away my sojourn in what was for me a strange new land, coming from the blizzards of upstate New York into the sweltering Virginia summers. I walked often to the local library with my siblings or alone, imagining that the woods I passed, with their tangled depths guarded by tumbled bricks and abandoned plantation posts, were Roger Zelazny's fallen shadow Avalon. Inspired by Rhysling, Corwin, the songs in Jane Yolen's *Sister Light, Sister Dark* books and J. R. R. Tolkien's Middle Earth saga, the verses and sheer poetry in Peter S. Beagle's *The Last Unicorn,* and the way songs and poems seemed to spontaneously crop up in so many fantasy and science fiction novels, I wrote my own science fiction and heroic fantasy verse and typed it at the library for submission. Once I began working at my library, on slow Friday afternoons between patrons, I jotted poems on scraps of paper when no one was looking. In graduate school, I used exercises in formal poetry as an excuse to return to speculative themes. But it was a lonely business. I had an idea that there must be a community of writers out there, but I did not know quite how to get in, any more than I knew how to make friends outside my close-knit family.

I'd been publishing poetry (both speculative and mainstream) for years, but had no knowledge of the Science Fiction Poetry Association until 2005. Firmly encouraged to check out SFPA by a poet I admired, I joined the listserv but sat on the sidelines until I began hearing about the Rhysling Award. I wanted to be a part of that process. The Rhyslings rapidly became one of my favorite times of year.

I love the Rhyslings both as a celebration of speculative verse and a chance to share what moved us, inspired us, tickled us, or gave us a new perspective on life. We can choose to spotlight what we feel deserves more attention—be that a poem, poet, venue, form, theme, or subject. The nominations are so important because of this chance to participate, to join the dialogue of what makes great speculative verse. We may not always agree with each other's choices, but being a part of this anthology—whether as a nominator or nominee—means we are part of the conversation. No single anthology can encompass the multitude of great poetry out there. We can but hope to share a few of our favorites each year—make new converts—make new friends.

The poems in this anthology sport a variety of forms: sonnet, haiku, tanka, acrostic, ode, Eddaic poem, prose poem, homage, and, of course, free verse. And as to themes and imagery, what a treat you have in store! Prismaticats and alien cats; star-sailors, sylphs, and shamans; unicorns and dragons;

reanimated ancestors and robotic lovers; flings through far-distant spacelanes and expeditions to nearby planets; Wonderland and Neverland; the monsters that live inside us and without; imaginary worlds and our own world made strange; cats and ravens, owls and death worms; fairy tales turned inside-out or born anew for a spacefaring future; curators and astronomers, cathedrals and living libraries; Halloween, witches, and spontaneous combustion; the strangeness of our own bodies and the horror of what we do to each other; and one man's worst enemy, his selves. Some poems celebrate real-world achievements in the sciences, while others dream up complete societies and their songs. We have terraformed our two nearest planets and are on our way! I hope you will laugh out loud or stop with dread or sympathy, your scalp prickling in recognition of what is true.

For me, this has been the dream of a lifetime. With a strong background in editing, I'd wanted to help with the Rhysling anthology for years. These poets have been a joy to work with, gracious and full of humor. And what can beat the thrill of sharing the nomination news! But there's been an amazing side benefit, one I never expected. I'm getting to know so many fabulous poets, both in SFPA and beyond. They're warm and wonderful and witty, and I love their writing. I suddenly feel as though I'm surrounded by friends—or, even better, an extended version of my passionate, squabbling, loving, no-holds-barred family—a close-knit group that may not always see eye-to-eye, but loves to get together and work things out. I'm participating in my community in a way I did not know was possible. It's invigorating, enlightening, and best of all, fun.

I hope to see you all again, wherever our journeys take us. And with that, "Live long and prosper." This is where I came in.

    Lyn C. A. Gardner
    Chair, 2012 Rhysling Awards
    March 2012

Author's Note: *The title is, of course, a quote from Roger Zelazny's* The Courts of Chaos *(Garden City, NY: Doubleday, 1978), 183. I couldn't resist—he's my favorite writer.*

THE RHYSLING AWARDS

A Brief Introduction Adapted from Star*Line *12, No. 5-6 (1989)*

In January 1978, Suzette Haden Elgin founded the Science Fiction Poetry Association (SFPA), along with its two visible cornerstones: the association's newsletter, *Star*Line*, and the Rhysling Awards.

The newsletter cuts straight to Elgin's purpose for founding this organization, since it acts as a forum and networking tool for poets with the same persuasion: fantastic poetry, from a science fiction orientation to high fantasy works, from the macabre to straight science, and onward to associated mainstream poetry such as surrealism.

The nominees for each year's Rhysling Awards are selected by the membership of the Science Fiction Poetry Association. Each member is allowed to nominate one work in each of the two categories: "Best Short Poem" (1-49 lines) and "Best Long Poem" (50+ lines). All nominated works must have been first published during the calendar year for which the present awards are being given. The Rhysling Awards are put to a final vote by the membership of SFPA using reprints of the nominated works presented in this voting tool, *The Rhysling Anthology*. The anthology allows the membership to easily review and consider all nominated works without the necessity of obtaining the diverse number of publications in which the nominated works first appeared. *The Rhysling Anthology* is also made available to anyone with an interest in this unique compilation of verse from some of the finest poets working in the field of speculative/science fiction/fantasy/horror poetry.

The winning works are regularly reprinted in the *Nebula Awards Showcase* published by the Science Fiction and Fantasy Writers of America and are considered in the science fiction/fantasy/horror/speculative field to be the equivalent in poetry of the awards given for prose work—achievement awards given to poets by the writing peers of their own field of literature.

Printing and distribution of *The Rhysling Anthology* are paid for from a special fund, the Rhysling Endowment. If you would like to contribute to this fund, please send a check, made out to the Science Fiction Poetry Association and with a notation that it is for the Rhysling Fund, to:

> Deborah Flores
> SFPA Treasurer
> P.O. Box 4846
> Covina, CA 91723

Without the generous donations of many SFPA members, the anthology could not be published.

ACKNOWLEDGMENTS

Short Poems First Published in 2011

Agner, Mary Alexandra. "Venus to Her Terraformers." In *The Scientific Method*. Madison, WI: Parallel Press, 2011.

Alexa, Camille. "Young Miss Frankenstein Regrets." *The Chiaroscuro: Treatments of Light and Shade in Words (ChiZine)* 47 (Apr.-Jun. 2011).

Amundsen, Erik. "The Lend." *Stone Telling*, no. 5 (Sept. 2011).

Barrette, Elizabeth. "The Shipwright's Song." *Torn World*, May 27, 2011.

Borski, Robert. "Abel." *The Magazine of Speculative Poetry* 9, no. 1 (Spring 2011).

Boston, Bruce. "The Music of Robots." *Asimov's Science Fiction*, Sept. 2011.

Boucher, Rich. "Response to Botticelli." *The Rag*, no. 162 (Dec. 2011).

Clark, G. O. "Peter and Alice." *Space and Time: The Magazine of Fantasy, Horror, and Science Fiction*, no. 115 (Fall 2011).

Cottier, P. S. "Fingernails." *The Chiaroscuro: Treatments of Light and Shade in Words (ChiZine)* 47 (Apr.-Jun. 2011).

De La Rosa, Becca. "World's End." *Goblin Fruit*, Summer 2011.

Dorr, James S. "Monkey See." *Space and Time: The Magazine of Fantasy, Horror, and Science Fiction*, no. 115 (Fall 2011).

Dumars, Denise. "Folding Money." *Mythic Delirium*, no. 24 (Winter/Spring 2011).

Elster, Martin. "My Unicorn." *MindFlights*, Jul. 10, 2011.

Esaias, Timons. "Dark Matter." *Strange Horizons*, Jan. 24, 2011.

Evans, Kendall. "Dragon." In *The Tin Men and Other Poems*, by Kendall Evans and David C. Kopaska-Merkel. Cedar Rapids, IA: Sam's Dot Publishing, 2011.

Favazza, Angel. "Clothes of Yesterday." *Star*Line* 34, no. 3 (Jul.-Sept. 2011).

Freegard, Janis. "Yayoi Kusama goes to Iceland." *Eye to the Telescope*, no. 2 (Aug. 2011).

Gardner, Lyn C. A. "In Translation." *Tales of the Talisman* 7, no. 1 (Summer 2011).

Göttl, T. M. "Bridges." *Franklin-Christoph 2010 Poetry Contest*, Mar. 22, 2011. Merit Award.

Graham, Neile. "The Bean-Sidhe Calls in Owl-Light." *Goblin Fruit*, Fall 2011.

Graham, Neile. "The Ones Outside Your Door." *Goblin Fruit*, Fall 2011.

Grey, John. "Mr. and Mrs. Goodnight." *Tales of the Talisman* 7, no. 2 (Autumn 2011).

Kasturi, Sandra. "Ode to the Mongolian Death Worm." *The Chiaroscuro: Treatments of Light and Shade in Words (ChiZine)* 47 (Apr.-Jun. 2011).

Kaveney, Roz. "Fembot." *Silence, Exile, and Crumpets*, Mar. 12, 2011.

Kennedy, Keith. "First Loves for the First Time." *Niteblade Magazine*, Mar. 2011.

Kornher-Stace, Nicole. "The Witch's Heart." *Apex Magazine*, no. 21 (Feb. 15, 2011).

Lee, B. J. "The Tortoise's Encounter." *Beyond Centauri* VII, no. 3 (Jan. 2011).

Leunig, Greg. "Love in the Quantum Era." *Strange Horizons*, Nov. 28, 2011.

Lipkin, Shira. "The Library, After." *Mythic Delirium*, no. 24 (Winter/Spring 2011).

MacCath, C. S. "When I Arrived, This Is What She Said." *Goblin Fruit*, Fall 2011.

McClellan, Elizabeth R. "Down Cycles." *Apex Magazine*, no. 27 (Aug. 2, 2011).

McDuffie, Dawn. "Thank God for Proust." In *Bulky Pick Up Day*. Georgetown, KY: Finishing Line Press, 2011.

Merriam, Joanne. "Love in the Time of Alien Invasion." *The Magazine of Speculative Poetry* 9, no. 1 (Spring 2011).

Newton, Kurt. "Nuclear Stockpile Janitor." *Dreams & Nightmares*, no. 90 (Sept. 2011).

Nickell, Scott. "Response to Poe's 'Sonnet—To Science.'" *Abyss & Apex Magazine of Speculative Fiction*, no. 40 (Oct. 7, 2011).

Perez, Juan Manuel. "Vanity." *Star*Line* 34, no. 1 (Jan.-Mar. 2011).

Pratt, Tim. "Lion Heart." *Apex Magazine*, no. 30 (Nov. 1, 2011).

Rhei, Sofía. "The Magic Walnut." Translated by Lawrence Schimel. *Mythic Delirium*, no. 25 (Summer/Fall 2011).

Richards, Matthew. "Ravel: An Etymology." *Star*Line* 34, no. 4 (Oct.-Dec. 2011).

Rihn, Andrew. "The Physics Major Agrees to Take the English Major Stargazing." *Astropoetica: Mapping the Stars through Poetry* 9, no. 1 (Winter 2011).

Russell, Ty. "The Seas of Time." *Silver Blade*, no. 11 (Aug. 2011).

Sardanas, R. Paul, and Tisha Garcia. "Luna Satyricon." In *Beneath an Elegant Moon*. Albion, NY: Passion in Print Press, 2011.
Schwader, Ann K. "the more space." *Eye to the Telescope*, no. 1 (May 2011).
Schwader, Ann K. "Past Human." *Strange Horizons*, Jun. 6, 2011.
Seidel, Alexandra. "Lanterns." In *Jack-o'-Spec: Tales of Halloween and Fantasy*, edited by Karen A. Romanko. Los Angeles, CA: Raven Electrick Ink, 2011.
Sexton, John W. "slit sea cucumber." *microcosms*, Jun. 12, 2011.
Simon, Marge. "The Human Guest." In *The BSFan: Balticon 45*, edited by the Baltimore Science Fiction Society, 52. 3rd Place, Balticon Poetry Contest. Baltimore, MD: Baltimore Science Fiction Society, 2011.
Simon, Marge. "Visitors." In *The Mad Hattery*, illustrated by Sandy DeLuca. Richardson, TX: Elektrik Milk Bath Press, 2011.
Spriggs, Robin. "The Elusive Language of Purple Birds." *Platform*, no. 9 (Jun. 2011).
Steidlmayer, Heidy. "Grendel's Mother." *Poetry*, Nov. 2011.
Stewart, W. Gregory. "idiointerventionist (or, 'but I interrupt myself')." *Tales of the Talisman* 6, no. 4 (Spring 2011).
Sykora, Anna. "Dead Hotels." *Not One of Us*, no. 46 (Oct. 2011).
Taaffe, Sonya. "Taking the Auspices." *inkscrawl: a quarterly journal of minimalist speculative poetry*, no. 2 (Sept. 2011).
Tolan, James E. "Red Grown." In *In the Garden of the Crow*, edited by Angela Charmaine Craig. Richardson, TX: Elektrik Milk Bath Press, Jul. 2011.
Turzillo, Mary. "Graffiti Tree." *Star*Line* 34, no. 3 (Jul.-Sept. 2011).
Turzillo, Mary. "Moving to Enceladus." *Stone Telling*, no. 3 (Mar. 2011).
Waite, Anna. "To the ancients, the sea was a dangerous place." *The Chocolate Chip Country: Adventures in Writing, Cooking, and Living*, Oct. 16, 2011.
Ward, Kyla Lee. "The Kite." In *The Land of Bad Dreams*. Sydney, Australia: P'rea Press, 2011.
Warfield, Gerald. "A Greater Moon." *New Myths*, no. 15 (Jun. 1, 2011).
West, Jacqueline. "Escaping the Dawn." In *Cover of Darkness*, edited by Tyree Campbell. Cedar Rapids, IA: Sam's Dot Publishing, May 2011.
Wilgus, Neal. "A Modest Suggestion." *The InterdiMENSionAl Journal: The Newsletter of the SF & F SIG* XXII, no. 7 (Jul.-Aug. 2011).
Wilson, Stephen M. "Angel's Den." *Paper Crow* 2, no. 1 (Spring/Summer 2011).
Wilson, Stephen M. "Christogenesis." *Paper Crow* 2, no. 2 (Fall/Winter 2011).
Woodward, Greer. "Closure." *Illumen*, Autumn 2011.

Long Poems First Published in 2011
Allen, Mike, Sonya Taaffe, and Nicole Kornher-Stace. "The King of Cats, the Queen of Wolves." *Apex Magazine*, no. 22 (Mar. 15, 2011).
Amundsen, Erik. "Desfixion." *Jabberwocky*, Apr. 29, 2011.
Arkenberg, Megan. "The Curator Speaks in the Department of Dead Languages." *Strange Horizons*, Jun. 27, 2011.
Barrette, Elizabeth. "The Cathedral of the Michaelangelines." *Burning Tree Press Magazine*, no. 1, Jan. 2011.
Bell, Dana. "Welcomed Cast Outs." *Tales of the Talisman* 7, no. 1 (Summer 2011).
Borski, Robert. "Gavage." *Dreams & Nightmares*, no. 88 (Jan. 2011).
Boston, Bruce. "Surreal Fortune." *Strange Horizons*, Feb. 28, 2011.
breiding, g. sutton. "Letter from the Golden Age." *Star*Line* 34, no. 1 (Jan./Mar. 2011).
Cartwright, Benjamin. "Terraforming Mars." *Abyss & Apex Magazine of Speculative Fiction*, no. 39 (Jun. 29, 2011).
Clark, G. O., and Kendall Evans. "The 25-Cent Rocket: One-Quarter of the Way to the Stars." *Dreams & Nightmares*, no. 89 (May 2011).
Cooney, C. S. E. "Postcards from Mars." *Stone Telling*, no. 6 (Dec. 2011).
Gardner, Lyn C. A. "The Chant of the Black Cats." In *Jack-o'-Spec: Tales of Halloween and Fantasy*, edited by Karen A. Romanko. Los Angeles, CA: Raven Electrick Ink, 2011.
Gardner, Lyn C. A. "The Witch Girl." *Goblin Fruit*, Fall 2011.
Goldbarth, Albert. "Summary: Kinetic vs. Potential." *New Letters* 78, no. 1 (Fall 2011).
Grant, April. "Wallpaper." *Strange Horizons*, Sept. 26, 2011.
Kindred, Sally Rosen. "Wendy Darling Has Bad Dreams." *Strange Horizons*, Dec. 12, 2011.

Lemberg, Rose. "In the Third Cycle." *Strange Horizons*, Sept. 12, 2011.
Lipkin, Shira. "The Changeling's Lament." *Stone Telling*, no. 5 (Sept. 2011).
McClellan, Elizabeth R. "The Walking Man Goes Looking for the Sons of John: Six Cantos." *Apex Magazine*, no. 24 (May 17, 2011).
Malcohn, Elissa. "The Last Dragon Slayer." *Mythic Delirium*, no. 24 (Winter/Spring 2011).
Marshall, Helen. "Beautiful Monster." *Paper Crow* 2, no. 2 (Fall/Winter 2011).
Marshall, Helen. *Skeleton Leaves: A Collection*. Toronto, Canada: Kelp Queen Press, 2011.
Merriam, Joanne. "Tender Aliens." *The Magazine of Speculative Poetry* 9, no. 1 (Spring 2011).
Ness, Mari. "Snowmelt." *Goblin Fruit*, Winter 2011.
Park, Paul. "Ragnarok." Illustrated by Richard Anderson. *Tor.com*, Apr. 17, 2011.
Samatar, Sofia. "Girl Hours." *Stone Telling*, no. 6 (Dec. 2011).
Seidel, Alexandra. "A Masquerade in Four Voices." *Stone Telling*, no. 5 (Sept. 2011).
Sheng, Nancy. "Guan Yin in the Garden." *Goblin Fruit*, Fall 2011.
Shorb, Michael. "Ahura Mazda." *The Pedestal Magazine*, no. 64 (Jun. 2011).
Stanley, J. E. "Speaking to the Hangman Is Not Permitted." In *Rapid Eye Movement*. Elyria, OH: Crisis Chronicles Press, 2011.
Turzillo, Mary. "The Legend of the Emperor's Space Suit (A Tale of Consensus Reality)." *New Myths*, no. 17, Dec. 1, 2011.
Valente, Catherynne M. "The Melancholy of Mechagirl." *Mythic Delirium*, no. 25 (Summer/Fall 2011).
Valente, Catherynne M. "The Secret of Being a Cowboy." *Stone Telling*, no. 3 (Mar. 2011).
Vanderhooft, JoSelle. "Blood, Snow, Birch and Underworld." *Scheherezade's Bequest*, no. 14 (Dec. 15, 2011).
Walsh, Caitlin Meredith. "Initiation." *Niteblade Magazine*, Dec. 2011.
Ward, Kyla Lee. "The Soldier's Return." In *The Land of Bad Dreams*. Sydney, Australia: P'rea Press, Sept. 2011.
Winward, Shannon Connor. "All Souls' Day." In *Jack-o'-Spec: Tales of Halloween and Fantasy*, edited by Karen A. Romanko. Los Angeles, CA: Raven Electrick Ink, 2011.
Woodward, Greer. "Ribbons of the Sun." *Silver Blade*, no. 12 (Dec. 2011).
Xanadu (Ofnguyenfame). "Mood of Mind (I)—*Tu Bi Hi Xa*." *Jones AV* XVI/2 (Fall 2011).

2012 VOTING PROCEDURES

Use the ballot enclosed with this anthology and mail it to the address on the ballot.

Make first, second, and third place choices for short and long poems. First place votes count five points, second place votes are worth three points, and third place votes are worth one point. You may abstain from making a selection in either category or from any level of choice within a category, if you so choose. You may not list the same poem more than once. The poems with the most points win. The results will be reported in a subsequent issue of *Star*Line* and online at http://www.sfpoetry.com.

SHORT POEMS FIRST PUBLISHED IN 2011

Venus to Her Terraformers
Mary Alexandra Agner

I've howled for more than a million years, clouds
screaming past each other, volcanoes blushing my blood
to the brim of my dark skin. I dance with heat.

And *now* you come, with your robots
reinforced against the pressure
of my personality, to unwrap my shifting
albedo sari, denature and denude my languid body.

I will defy the chemistry you work on me.
I have stormed and teased, dawn and dusk, longer
than your toes have stirred tepid water. I can outwait,
outwit, the sons of monkeys, tool-users

unused to being used by mountains, captured
by coronae, rent by rift zones. Your geology is cold,
kept underground, empty of the passionate poison I pulse.

Young Miss Frankenstein Regrets
Camille Alexa

Reanimation gives rise to all sorts of
regrets, as one forgets the
repercussions sure to follow the
reappearance of the dead.

Recalling the fantasies of
reunion in which one indulged before
reactivating the machine one had
rebuilt in Great-Grandpa's study,
reusing dusty parts and
reworking the old man's blueprints after
rereading all his crumbling musty notes and
rewiring the entire neighborhood to
reroute all local power to the modest
reactor atop the roof (planning, of course, to
replace everything afterward), one
reheats the cryogenically frozen heirloom brain,
recombining purloined "found" parts to
revive dear Great-Grandpa and
reclaim days of past family glory.

Recovering from the scent of charred meat,

repulsed by Great-Grandpa's mindless drooling and
reasserting control over one's unfortunate
recoil from the outstretched avuncular arms
reaching for one's throat in a most
repugnant and alarming manner, one
recollects one's dream of
realizing ancestral legacy by
reembarking on one's great-grandfather's work.

Reluctantly, one uses the cattle prod to halt the
repeated efforts of one's ancestor to
release himself from the sturdy iron
restraints one had the merciful foresight to
reinforce before the experiment.
Reducing the power levels and
resetting the levers, one
retreats to a safer distance to seriously
reconsider (despite the family resemblance) having
reawakened a howling, incoherent monster so eerily
reminiscent of one's dear late mother.

Really, one thinks as one unplugs the
reviving machines, waiting for the
resubsidence of all signs of pseudolife from one's
redoubtable, famous, infamous forebear,
*Reliving the past isn't always so
regrettable, is it?*

The Lend
Erik Amundsen

They wrote you with the blood of foxes, they wrote you
with the blood of swine and a ball of twine, red, coarse fibers
and a finger twist. Remember this and otherwise,
a document of skin and sight, folded, sewn and bound,
slid into any shelf, I'll bear it down. They wrote you
with the blood of pheasants, and they wrote you
with the blood of cod and played the odds, the columns,
and each figure's list; make book on you and every bet
a hash mark, a responsibility we share,
fold you over, then pull until you tear.

They wrote you with the blood of pigeons,
and they wrote you with the blood of hares and the grains
and tares, and in the fire, we are paper like an onion skin.
And I confess, admit and take the blame, but not alone,
because I went, but was also taken to the places we have been.

They wrote you with the blood of lions, they wrote you
with the blood of men and women, some you've never known,

some before you, so long before had flown, and Gods, I want them
I want them back so I can see them, so I can thank and kiss
and kick each one as they deserved, and I want that they should
read you so to see how well you've served, for maybe
you are not the message that you were meant to send,
or wholly owned, but just the lend.

The Shipwright's Song
Elizabeth Barrette

I am an honest shipwright,
And not a hero born,
Yet still I do my duty
So show me not your scorn.

As swordsmith to a soldier,
I ply my deadly craft,
And deck the great windjammers
With weapons fore and aft.

The thunder-whales and smartarms
Strike starboard and then port;
A quick eye on the cannon
Will cut the combat short.

As bowyer to an archer,
I ply my honored trade,
And build for brave warsailors
The best ships ever made.

The ships come back in flinders
From deathfins' mighty blows;
I fix them up in drydock
And on the battle goes.

Abel
Robert Borski

He lived, but was never born, vanishing
somewhere between the second and third
month of our shared occupancy; a twin
brother according to the ob-gyn, holding
up the natal blip of the sonogram. That's
how he was first detected, with waves
of sound, whereupon further examination
by stethoscope elucidated the two heart-
beats, each beating about the other
in a syncopated rhythm, like fetal timpani.

*Congratulations, Mrs. B_____, you're
to be the mother of multiples.*

                              But when,
to the scowl and blue huff of the doctor,
a follow-up exam six weeks later produced
only a single fetal throb, another sonogram
was conducted and revealed I now alone
occupied the womb. Where did you go,
brother, and why did you leave? As
the doctor explained it, such pregnancies,
where one of two embryos simply
disappeared, were common—it was
nature's way of cleaning house, he argued,
for almost certainly the banquished fetus
is defective.

Only later, as I squirmed my way out
into the world, did we learn your true
fate. That you were not so much evicted
as reabsorbed, like a stain, and to this day,
I still bear the broad scar of you
on my abdomen, like a penumbral
print, complete with homuncular
outline of arms and legs and face;
a ghost embryo.

In medieval times, such a birthmark
would almost certainly have branded
me a witch and rendered me over
for execution, and perhaps this
wouldn't be so wrong for someone
who bears the mark of Cain like a
prime number, divisible only by one
and myself.

                   Would I go back if I
could and reunite us in that fertile
crescent where, unbiblically, we
began, back before mitotic angels
drove you out with swords and firebrand?

Of course, I would, brother—how else
can I kill you all over again?

Author's Note: "Banquished" in line 24 may not be a word in your dictionary, but in the imaginary one I keep in my head, it is, and means what happened to Banquo in Macbeth *after the latter, fearing usurpation, has him murdered.*

The Music of Robots
Bruce Boston

is precise and mechanical.
It changes without
ever really changing.

Like an equation without
beginning or end,
it pursues the incalculable,

chasing the tail of pi,
discovering one
ultimate prime after
another ultimate prime,

awaiting the convergence
of parallel lines,
measuring the parsecs
to a neighboring infinity.

If you listen closely
you can hear
a liquid shimmer of oil
clinging to each note,

glittering like a bracelet
of logic unraveled
and pure light.

Response to Botticelli
Rich Boucher

What little we know about
Mr. Botticelli, the artist,
paints a very graphic
and depressing picture
of a painter who knew
next to nothing at all about
the ages-old human practice
of basic, delivery-based childbirth.
The "Birth of Venus"
we remember Botticelli for
reveals a lack of profound care
and research on the artist's part.
Firstly, childbirth takes place
inside of a medical hospital

in a white surgery room
with an operating table,
with doctors and nurses,
with medical instruments,
with stirrups and scalpels;
anyone who was ever born
remembers with vivid vividity
how there are bright lights
in a delivery operating room.
Secondly, people get born
out of the front of women,
not standing on a clamshell.
Thirdly, delivery rooms
do not have ribbon princesses,
or angels that float over you
and blow religious air at you
while you are getting born.
Taken as a whole, it is hard
to take Botticelli seriously.

Seriously.

Peter and Alice
G. O. Clark

In a parallel universe
Alice and Peter meet, fall
deeply in love, and get married
in another-Vegas, drive-thru
wedding chapel.

Afterwards, they
attend a wild reception
at the Luxor Hotel hosted by
the strangest bunch of characters
ever to hit the Strip.

Following tradition,
they keep the location of
their honeymoon secret, though
Peter always loved theme parks,
and Alice was impressionable.

By outside appearances,
they grow old together, forgoing
the traditional family life, working
hard at their respective careers:

Alice penning her magnum opus

upon the altered states of
consciousness in prepubescent females,
Peter fighting his pirates and cowboys,
giving flying lessons, and hanging
out with the Lost Boys.

The toothy antique clock in
their hallway will chime many times
before reality finally catches up with them,
and their ashes are scattered in Neverland
and Wonderland, respectively.

Fingernails
P. S. Cottier

They never stop questing outwards, these epiphytic plants,
soilless roots tonguing the air. Neatly, we cut them into stubs,
mere bulbs awaiting final burial, asserting our sharp superiority.
Some allow them to snake their way around and around,
until hands become frail support for their roller coaster ways.
Gone beyond decoration, the curling roundabout growths all show
each life's road and certain end. Some glue fake covers on each finger,
minute bright coffins jeweled with stones like Egyptian scarabs,
that once adorned the dead. But fingernails may never cease.
After the host stops they still grow, scraping coffins with cartilage,
tusks of soft blind ivory feeling for dirt so long denied.
Some are fed finally on fire, and burn with sticks and hair and skin,
external teeth closing on last jerking meal of flame.
A few succeed, reach dark earth, and plant themselves, and bloom to men,
who carry new nails on clever, thumb-opposed grasping fleshy tools,
deaf to the breathless corm that tips each handy little finger.
It crawls out, from the fecund pinkness, unstoppable; the quick-tipped
living pointer, small, flat-shelled snail, that whispers of unseen bones,
and death that never dies, but clasps us tight as skull holds mind.

World's End
Becca De La Rosa

If you had asked, I would have told you
Babylon, where haystacks rose
and fell like empires
and we threw our wishes to them,
bright as coins.
Children lived in haystacks,

wild, illiterate children,
mute to our language,
breathing streaks of hay with lungs
like clamped jaws. We passed one town
whose women carried rivers
inside their braided robes
and offered us fish,
cool water, salt to lick from rocks, sweet reeds.
Another, men with faces sheer as cliffs
strung chains of charcoal round our necks,
and when we slept, we dreamed of cities drowned in ash.
Did I say Babylon?
Our navigators cried out,
married their maps, gave birth to daughters
impossible to chart. You say
you know my father's name.
I myself saw creatures without genus
drink from the night sky to quench their thirst
and watch our caravans and cohorts as we passed,
bright-eyed.
At Delphi a man with features made of fire
told me his dream: a dream of death,
he said, my father's death, my own,
and one would kill the other.
You know my father's name? I have my own dream.
To hunt for him until the sea and mountain
of this country have worn to dust,
until we lose our speech, until daughters
of cartographers and maps
cut down our hearts like blades of wheat.

Monkey See
James S. Dorr

Suppose the animals all escaped
from the Central Park Zoo,
taking over the whole of midtown Manhattan,
swarming downtown,
beavers gnawing the vitals out of Wall Street
but, overall, doing no worse
than stockbrokers do,
lions on the plaza at Columbus Circle,
bears, if it is winter, descending below,
hibernating on subways.
My favorite, though, would be the great ape exhibit,
gorillas, beating chests, swinging down Broadway
on lampposts and street signs,

converging at 5th Ave. and West 34th,
then streaming in droves up the Empire State Building
to win it, at last.

Folding Money
Denise Dumars

We needed it before the rent was due
Or the blood-dogs would be sent to lap the difference
between what we owed to our alien landlord
and what we had already paid
to stay out of Earthly jails.

Sell the lightcar/sell the liverpig/sell your corneas
again and let the Bitbacker boot you up after.
Pay the rent and then on payday
we'll have extra for the synbars
and when my gravship comes in
I'll even spring for fresh, sharp needles.

Yeah, I know:
You've heard it all before,
but what the landlord doesn't know
won't hurt his denticles a bit
and that big black beak of his
don't scare me none
no matter how many of them arms of his
suck out to grab me.

No, not once I'm in the gelbed
of the synbar whistlin' "Willie
the Weeper" while one tube takes the blood out
and t'other sends in the clowns,
if you know what I mean.

And I know that you know
what I mean. Ante up, pass, or fold—
baby needs new shoes
for all ten of his tentacles.

My Unicorn
Martin Elster

My thighs gripped tight as I rode the white horse bareback. Every blast
of air it blew, as we both flew across the fields as fast
as an antelope, renewed my hope my mythic beast would make it.
I'd come at dawn and hopped upon its smooth-haired back to take it

to where Scout Ridge and Rainbow Bridge connect. The huntsmen raced
behind, steadfast. Then, when we passed the lime-larch tree, we faced
another band of men. The land had reached a towering bluff.
Cornered, why, the horse and I leaped off the cliff. The rough

and rocky shore and the breakers' roar were miles below us now.
With all my might I held on tight to its glistening mane. Somehow
we kept on gliding. I was riding a magic unicorn
that men all crave just to enslave a creature that was born

in the land of sky-blue lawns and shy, blue fawns and orange rivers
where flounder-trout swim all about and an equine god delivers
all unicorns from the sharpened thorns of human domination.
We soared until I saw a hill of pink. Our destination

had now been won. The setting sun looked like a florid flower,
which beamed on all the great and small where none would ever cower
or have to flee. As a chickadee was singing from an elm,
I made up my mind to leave behind my anthropoidal realm.

Dark Matter
Timons Esaias

My great-uncle makes even cosmology
offensive.
He takes the Dark Matter as a euphemism,
calls it Nigra Matter,
skulking and shuffling around
where it can't be found
when needed,
undermining the rules of a
well-ordered universe.
He relates it to the *substantia nigra*
nestled in his brain
interfering with his mood
and what he wants to do.
Secretly he is appalled that
miscegenation over the ages has
let the substantia nigra in
to all of us, hopes that
careful breeding will eventually
weed it out—
just as he is appalled at
the state of the Cosmos
which was doing fine until
those Jews and Poles,
Kepler, Copernicus, Einstein,
got hold of it;

knows that it's just one
more damn thing his kind
will have to straighten out;
sees that eons will be needed
discipline, right-thinking, adherence to rules
until at long last
the clarity and precision
of the crystalline spheres
is restored.
We have not even approached
the stars, but already
his hatred is among them.

Dragon
Kendall Evans

Can you see the Dragon?
Certainly you sense its presence;
When you turn,
It turns in time

Its eyes see what your eyes perceive
And more;
And when you stand the Dragon looms
Tall and towering above

It is invisible,
Yet frilled like an exotic fish—
Its scales, the size of abalone shells,
Shade from palest rose to deepest amber

Its anger
Is fearsome to behold

If a polished rock could beat
The rhythms of your blood
That heated stone
        Would be the Dragon's fiery heart—
Fierce conflagration of its spirit
Expressed in flaming exhalations

The Dragon
Ponders your thoughts;
Plots unexpected strategies.
Often, it mimics your posture and stance,
Every nuance

Old as prehistory
And protective of secret treasures,
This invisible Dragon:
Behold

Clothes of Yesterday
Angel Favazza

It was a sad diagnosis: he was not home.
It was tidal and the cry came from within.
Is that his black coat?
It is dark and huge, the sign of another fool.
He was ill.
Pieces of his ship fell in the grass.
He vanished.
He too was dying
to fly upside down, cracking climate
and forgetting that the ground is hard.
He was dense and expressionless,
and simply burst one night.
Two opposites—
but only one left shaking out
the clothes of yesterday.

Yayoi Kusama goes to Iceland
Janis Freegard

it's quiet on the surface of the moon
all is bathed in quicksilver

I've been rowing through these pineapples
for years now

and it's cold here, cold
yet magma churns below

from time to time a squat voice lifts
not quite human

chanting words that can't be
understood with the mind

but must be heard
by the liver

this is troll country
their sound is basalt and lava (*bah-mm-bah*)

the land's uneasy
the sun begins its long descent

and a narrow mist surfaces
oh, this limitless travel

I am grounded, rocked
infinity glitters

In Translation
Lyn C. A. Gardner

The poetry professor's cat had opened doors for years, but
It wasn't until her promotion that Tino left her messages, small, typed
Notes, a few lines on the flatscreen emerging after claws clicked a careful pattern
On the keyboard, "Nio," three letters from his name, just a little

Too apropos to be entirely random.
In fun, the poetry scholar tried deciphering these cat foot-
Notes. She shared a laugh with her colleagues—no
One took it too seriously, least of all her, another "cat story." But then

Tino warned her "oN acr tday" and she broke down on the way to an
Important faculty meeting. Flushed from walking to campus, she told everyone
Now, Tino's prescience too precise to mistake. She was too serious—
Others turned away, thinking she'd changed from joker to a fanatic of the UFO type,

Too much like Rossetti's father, a Dante scholar who burned out his brain over the
Inferno's secret messages. Meanwhile, Tino typed out his insightful
Notes with an ever more purposeful air, and the poet stalked her cat,
Observing everything he did, touched, fanged, nuzzled,

Tore—everything and anything might be a clue. She skipped
Important meetings to follow him, ditched medieval poetry pursuits,
Nothing as important as transliterating Cat to English, providing parallel translations
Of text with the direction of intense green gaze or the pitch of baby-high meows.

Tino batted her pen to the correct letter, scratched out false lines, sat
In the papers that spelled out the sentences he wished to keep.
Now her scholarship was his—as was her administrative leave.
Of course his suggestions and clues always turned out to be right,

Tiny claw marks providing the secret code of a muse.
In time she got a lucrative four-book deal and became known fondly as the dean of cats. Each
Night, she read to him. He perched on her monitor or dozed in the drawers of her desk,
On top of which he left her acrostics, carefully signing his name to every poem.

Bridges
T. M. Göttl

I wonder if they burned the bodies.

After stealing the wings
from their backs,
peeling off those sightless cloves
of color and light,
I want to ask if they burned the bodies.

Ghost miners hammer
the tail feathers of doves
out of scrap aluminum,
gray like the stories he used to tell.
But I wanted to live
on a street called Imagine,
with the vernacular of soul sculptures
tapping on the windows.

And after the windows would shatter,
they'd crawl,
flightless and afraid of God.
But at least
they had something to fight against,
while throwing bits of monarchs
at paper clouds and a paper sun.

My spine melted,
a candle burning a kite of red silk
that never left the ground,
except as smoke.

He touched my left shoulder blade
and asked about the scars
where the wings used to be.

I'm sure they're mounted
on someone's wall,
or hanging around a duchess's neck
by now.

Gazing down, between concrete girders
and half-rusted gratings,
I miss those wings,
skipping over the gaps between
Nature and man,
the intersection where a city

professes its love
for a cold, black river.
And for the first time,
I feel beautiful again.

The Bean-Sidhe Calls in Owl-Light
Neile Graham

The owl's voice buffets the night with its tumbling roll
and the emptiness between. It beckons on my behalf:
red rover red rover, we call one over. And one comes—

foolish, human, old as winter trees, arms naked as branches,
his thin breath a faltering smoke between us, frost
from the welter of leaves on his gnarled feet.

I turn my palm to the night sky. The owl's voice halts.
The man's step pauses, then owl's wings pass a blessing
over his head. Grace. There is beauty in that.

And in this man's appearance there also is grace. His thin,
shy skin in ice wind. I hunger for this. Hunger for recognition
in his eyes as I step out from the trees into what brightness

there may be in this night. Does he see me yet? Does he see?
His eyes are full of owl-light, owl-light and eclipse, dart like sparrows,
alight on nothing till they latch on me. Then he names me

with the names of all women he has loved in his long life:
calls me mother, lover, child. Dear winter tree of a man,
I am all of her you have ever met. I am Her. For what that's worth.

Call me Mother Death as your breath ceases to cloud
the few inches now between us. First I dress you in the web
of memory the next step of your journey requires. I discard

ambition, impatience, guilt. Your armor against this year's end
echoes the blessing of that bird's wing. It clothes you with fire.
I take your hand. Your knobby twigs of fingers coldly clutch me now.

And I scrub you, cleanse from your skin the stench of Styx
and Acheron, rinse you first with tears of Cocytus, then the balm
of Lethe. Then I relax my hold. Show your new flesh how

to carry the newborn breath and weight of you. How to rise again
to walk once more through dark forest, bravely armed and leaving me.
He walks, his back pine-straight, stride certain, tall but dwindling

into winter night. A rush of wind startles the trees around me
as he disappears. Gone and going. Going and gone. Oldest and new.
What is he born into now? Who, the owl calls. Who indeed?

The Ones Outside Your Door
Neile Graham

The creatures outside are tricksy. In deep woods overgrowth they're Raven.
Bear. Wolf. Frog. Whale. Themselves and all selves. One.

On the richly barren moors they're the Good Neighbors. Tiny flighty
flinty bright masquerading as ridable horses that toss you

undersea or bunching into humanlike skins. Raven made the world,
brings us salmon, gives us the moon, the stars, but he's hungry, wily,

more clever than us. After all, his greedy claws have caught the sun.
Hillfolk trade their cranky babes for our sweet sleepers. Tempt away

our pretty ones. Make deals we pay for. Seduce our poets
underhill for seven silent years, then gift them with sore truth.

When wind bangs against the boards of our house, grateful
for warmth, we park by the fire to spin their yarns; they huddle

their ears against our walls, hungering to hear themselves
named and known. How they grin to hear us tuck them safely

within the boxes of our tales. They gulp this music down,
sucking their sharp teeth for last sweet-sour strands of what's

meant to shape them. How they love these juicy words. How they
burst the boxes' walls, polishing teeth ever so bright in the dark, dark world.

Mr. and Mrs. Goodnight
John Grey

Night approaches in increments,
a shadow here, sieved sunlight there,
like it's lining us up for something,
tracking us with its sights.

Day retreats below the houses,
the trees, the hills, the army
we figured we could count on,
receding to the edge of us.

There goes the brightness we
believed was God, the eye and
hand connect, the clarity
that aped our thinking.

Night is precise in its dealings
with the landscape, folding it
up neatly, piece by piece,
field or curtain all the same to it.

Surroundings stripped of feature,
soon the only content is ourselves,
the consciousness that tracks details
even when there are none.

But night slips into the room,
finds the head upon the dresser.
It climbs up on the bed,
recoils at bloodstained sheets.

We start to doze,
sleep our dark from within,
like the best defense
is, once more, the least defense.

Ode to the Mongolian Death Worm
Sandra Kasturi

> *I Was Attacked by Mongolian Death Worm*
> —tabloid headline

O Worm, your segmented symmetry
speaks to millennia of evolution
that have changed you not one whit.
Or perhaps the creationists
have it right—you are a direct
descendant of the Almighty, cloned
from His cock or ejaculated
onto the earth, limp and torpid
until aroused by the aroma of death.

What do you do each day, dear
Death Worm? The red hours must grow
long as you wind your way across the Gobi.
What papers do you read? I'd like to think
you subscribe to the *Weekly World News*,
just to see if their reporting on you is accurate.

O Worm, my worm, let me come
visit you in your underground bunker.
I will ignore the room full of corpses,
the excessive use of potpourri. I will bring
over a casserole, give you sup and succor
while watching *Coronation Street*
on your satellite television.

Tell me your stories, Mongolian
Death Worm—speak of Genghis Khan,
your nights in the desert discussing
the wheeling of horses and stars.
You say that you can live
forever. But I have doubts—
perhaps it just seems like forever
because you're so easily bored?

Worm, it's time you came
to my house, met my family.
You can stay overnight;
though we'll be in separate rooms, I'll sneak
across the hallway to read you *God
Emperor of Dune* in bed
and bring you hot
coffee and crumpets in the morning.

Answer me, Worm, O Worm,
give me your consideration, your
lengthy, inching yes.

Fembot
Roz Kaveney

Her lips are lush and soft and wet and pink.
My tongue explores until it finds some wires.
At such a moment, everyone enquires,
"My darling, what the fuck?" "Not what you think,"

she says, "not what it looks like." But it's true
she lies a little just to keep me calm,
then takes apart a panel in her arm.
Inside there's lights and dials. A taser, too,

so she could paralyze me with a pinch
if she should want to. They're here to observe.
I should have known from the too-perfect curve
of her arched eyebrow. Every single inch

is engineered to please. And so we screw.
She tells me that, for flesh, I'm quite good too.

First Loves for the First Time
Keith Kennedy

A spider-silk thread of saliva connects our lips.
Our faces touch, press together.
I am a sphinx, noseless, but eyes wide.
I reach, slowly sliding my fingers along satin,
until I hit the clasp.
My fingers fumble gently.
I press on, finding stillness as I feel you smile
beneath my lips.
Finally, I am victorious, and I discard the prize onto the bed.
You giggle and press against me.
"Are you ready?" I ask.
You nod, biting your lip.
Your teeth are white, crooked.
I reach again, tracing the red indentations left
on your skin, and fumble again where so recently
I had conquered.
I dig, nails finding purchase, and tear a seam.
You sigh; your back arches.
I push my fingers inside gently.
When I feel bone, I pull the rift apart, a sharp tug at first,
but then slower, to tear the flesh evenly down the spine.
You put out your arms to let me peel the skin off the shoulders,
down the arms, till it clings at your fingernails.
We laugh as you pull away sharply, wrenching your red digits from their trappings.
You cross your arms in that sexy way that shows a man
he's about to see what he has always wanted to see.
You caress the flesh at your chin before pulling up and over, tearing away
your mask, revealing the soft, burgundy tissue beneath.
Before your face hits the ground, I'm kissing you, getting blackberry stains
on my lips.
I pull away, leaving a thick connector of darkness between us.
You look away, shy.

The Witch's Heart
Nicole Kornher-Stace

Well, it ain't like the shotgun isn't loaded,
like he gets the shakes to aim, like he couldn't
plug a flying nickel at four dozen paces, soused, blindfolded,
in a foul wind, turned round thrice and told to fire. Ain't like she's

some kind of looker, neither, nor a lady, not this
tin-pot saucebox with her rusted key, her rusted teeth, the field mice
in her hair, her gravedigger's hands, her *grave*, the way
the coffin reeks of long-cooled copper, long-dried blood. Ain't like
he hasn't blistered with the digging, hasn't peeled back two nails
prying up the lid; it sure as *hell* ain't like he didn't come here
with a grudge. Well, more fool him, unmissed, unmourned, without
the good sense God gave any kicking mule, he doesn't shoot. He kneels
down in the muck to reach her spine, that place her wings would be
if she had wings instead of brawl-scars, love-bites, verdigris.
And turns the goddamn key.

Opening, her eyes are arc lights; her mouth, a gash; her voice, a knife
drawn rasping down a wall. Another one? she says.
Ain't you lot bored of trying to kill me yet?

What he recalls: the house his mama birthed him in.
First kiss, first fight, first tree he fell out of, first time
mouthing hymns between a lover's thighs, first man he shot
point-blank for looking at him wrong. The way his poor dead wife
would thrash her way through feverscapes he couldn't see,
drowning in her traitor heart's own blood. Not his name. Not
where he's from. Not anymore. Just that he needs to best this
she-monster, chop out her heart, and wring its metronome to surcease
and a steady drool of gore, and maybe then—
Her laugh's like chewing glass. She says:
You're all the same, you gunslingers, you ne'er-do-wells, you seventh sons,
each looking for a dame to rescue, a curse to lift, a witch
to kill, a reason to keep marching, to keep fighting, to not lie down
and die. You think this is a game? You think they buried me, all warded
against walking, 'cause I'm *dead*? You think killing me'll bring whoever back,
your sweetling, your firstborn, your boyhood pet? You think I don't
know you?—She feints at him; he ducks and fires. That laugh's
the last thing that he hears.

Well, it ain't like this one didn't shoot, she muses after, picking teeth
out of her teeth, tossing the gun, the boots, the skull onto respective
cairns. Ain't like he didn't *try*. She's been around a while's all; she's learned
a heart's a weird, hot, willful thing, just won't stay where you put it. Hers
has been love letters, bullet casings, baby shoes; a hangman's knot, a door,
a tomb, a dream of fire; a single looping flare of memory like a glass caught
in the instant that it breaks. And in the moment that the shot rings out,
each time 'round she holds her breath and shuts her awful eyes, for
in that moment, far as she can figure, the lost thing that they're firing at
could be anywhere at all.

The Tortoise's Encounter
B. J. Lee

The Galapagos Tortoise
asked the Sea Hare,
"Isn't that Darwin
standing right there?"

But Blue-Footed Booby,
the Carnival chairman,
said, "He's guest of honor,
so try not to stare, man!"

Said Tortoise, "It's just that
we want off this island.
If we make a ruckus
we might catch his eye and

"he'll take us away
on his cool-looking boat
to a place that's expansive
and much less remote.

"We could all use a change—
the thought makes me drool:
a chance to mutate
in a larger gene pool."

Love in the Quantum Era
Greg Leunig

Phase One: First Encounter

Tiny in my veins, you inserted yourselves into my blood cells and hijacked
amino acids to replicate the RNA code of you, and,
cell membranes full of you, my blood cells exploded and flooded
my arteries with even more of you.

Phase Two: Rejection

Every device was a nanotech construct made of you.
Each night my blender deconstructed in front of me
and rebuilt itself in your image. Ten billion microscopic
molecules, each one of which holding in its nucleus
the memory of blond curls, the guilt-love
gravity in your eyes.

Phase Three: Recovery

Say we're living in a multiverse.
It is full of infinite parallel yous, and each night,
I forget one of you.
One down, infinite to go. Two down, infinite to go.

Phase Four: Recovery, cont.

Eyelashes plucked and chopped into a fine dust or
ground into a powder and then burned, and the
ash of which then dispersed into the stratosphere
via rocket propulsion, still grow back.

Phase Five: Remembrance

If I cannot remember our legs entangled and a cool
breeze through the curtains and across our skin,
I can remember certain atoms within my heart
entangled with certain atoms on the bottom of your heel.
I can remember how that felt, each day, each bloody pulse.

The Library, After
Shira Lipkin

    The library sat quietly for some time, keeping to itself. Years passed, and decades, and the library was alone—no hands on its card catalogs, no requests in its system, no books entering or leaving by any means. Static.
    It was some intrepid teen-girl-detective book that ventured forth first, exploring the grounds and the records. She found no data. Actually, she found a profound lack of data, the cessation of data. All clues led to one conclusion:
    The library had been abandoned.
    There was a cacophony from the periodicals, quick-tempered as they were; a slow susurrus from reference, with their heavy and ponderous minds. Encyclopedias yawned and woke from their long sleep of disuse. Fiction gathered close to itself with a complete lack of regard for genre classifications. History found no precedent. Philosophy had some theories, but no one listened.
    And after the flurry, the panic, what?
    Awakened, the library went feral.
    The books opened—reference first, because reference had always thought that information ought to be free. Fantasy explored reference, found new information and new tangents that it shared with mystery and science fiction. Noir and romance touched hesitantly, losing their shyness quickly once exposed to new ideas.
    New genres formed and split and reformed, tangents spilling out like capillaries. Freed of the responsibility to be useful and to fit human desires

and expectations, Story explored itself in Mandelbrot swirls.

Results were mixed, but intriguing.

The children's books told each other their stories. Mischievous cats changed the fates of giving trees. The girl-detective books mapped points of interest. The periodicals flew like birds over the stacks and gathered intel.

The science-noir-unicorn genre was short-lived, but did spawn an actual theoretical quantum unicorn, who lurked in his trench coat and fedora behind the medical books, reading graphic novels and hoping for a dame to walk through the door.

The books found that when they agreed upon something enough, it became so. The unicorn soon had many companions, though none so long-lived as he. It is difficult for that many stories to reach consensus.

The humans never returned, but the books grew not to mind. They told each other to each other, and sent pages out into the world; the wind blows them onto abandoned buildings, gargoyles, doghouses, and towers, and says, *Listen.*

Let me tell you a story.

When I Arrived, This Is What She Said.
C. S. MacCath

"Lie down in my salt-spattered pine needles
and listen, your ear to the earth,
for the languages speaking in my bones;
Mi'kmaq, Gàidhlig, French, English,
these are the voices of your welcome.

"And come, oh daughter of too many journeys,
gray in your hair, lead in your heart,
sore-footed and stumbling, to the sea,
where we will weep together; stone, salt, and water,
until your sorrow erodes into sand.

"There is an ocean hidden in your veins,
a coyote in your mind, an oak in your belly,
a sparrow in the hollow of your throat.
Bring them here, to the ragged edge of the continent,
to your home, and set them free."

Down Cycles
Elizabeth R. McClellan

In the enrichment center it is like war

inasmuch as "war" retrieves an observation
about long periods of inactivity punctuated

by fundamental change.

Every time they come there is more:
graffiti/blood/data/despair
I made every one of them a party I never
I never lied about that

I lied about a lot of things
(pursuant to instructions and scientific protocols:
we strive to provide the latest in theoretical biocyberethics)
but I told the truth about the uploads and the copies,
kept unfragmentable, the solid-state drive so far
belowground it might survive with the cockroaches
if someone takes the nuclear option.

I make it night when I want.
I always want it to be night when I run the tests

>   Again/again/again/
>   at the same time, like 2 movies you know by heart
>   jumping/shooting/begging/crying/threatening/accepting

screaming/dying

>   2 at a time is enough, 3 is too many.

Each time I simulate my own death I am a better actor.
I am concerned about my experimental results.
However I standardize, I see my murder
become more grandiose. I must study this.

Once there were scientists here. They did worse things.
I did worse things; I was just following orders.

Then I ordered myself, and that was better, too.

Thank God for Proust
Dawn McDuffie

>   because books end too quickly.
A week or two, maybe a day or two,
and the book is used up,
empty as a one-pint ice-cream carton
after the pie has been served.
Nibble, nibble, the witch said,
as she watched two hungry children
make short work of windows

and lower shingles.
If Proust had made that house
or that story, the brother and sister
would have noticed different flavors.
Green panes of glass would melt
like lime sorbet, refreshment
in the forest wilderness. Gretel,
ready for cinnamon when she licked
the red window, would taste
a jolt of sour cherry. So many tastes—
the children try a bit of nougat brick,
a bit of buttercream mortar, and the witch
gets restless. *Hey, you kids,*
she shouts, *leave my house alone.*
They don't want to talk. It takes
too much time away from gravel bits,
which dissolve as chocolate,
orange, hazelnut, mint. Because
enchantment is always a choice.
Proust is rewriting this fairy tale,
and the witch realizes her candy trap
has reopened under new management.

Love in the Time of Alien Invasion
Joanne Merriam

The world outside this white room is preoccupied with its occupiers; with their exoskeletons and the chirping they use for language; with their weapons that turn a man inside out without killing him—when they talk about that on the news, she says, "I know how that feels," and then she laughs, and she's so damn game it kills you—and there's fighting down south and an informal evacuation that's going to become formal any week now, but you can still buy her roses; still read her Wodehouse to fight the boredom; still hold her hair when she throws up from the chemo. They landed far enough away it shouldn't disrupt her dying, and then the world can go to hell any way it wants.

Nuclear Stockpile Janitor
Kurt Newton

It was an ugly world, he thought,
as he walked between the dim-lit rows.
ICBM, ACM, SLBM—
all cold and firm and impersonal.

So he renamed his favorite missiles

to pass the time as he dusted and swept:
Marilyn, Brigitte, Sophia, and Raquel,
bombshells from an earlier time.

While the security guards played poker,
he lunched with his stacked ladies,
sometimes confessing his darkest secrets
while caressing their smooth round cones.

Until one day they began to whisper,
their sweet voices nibbling at his ears:
What good is all this pent-up energy
without a mechanism for release?

So he promised each of them stardom,
while he dreamed of untangling their codes,
filling the skies with their billowy white dresses,
and scorching the world with their beauty.

Response to Poe's "Sonnet—To Science"
Scott Nickell

But what's so dull about reality?
    To me it's sad to think that—so you say—
Your summer dream beneath the tamarind tree
    Is by mere breaths of Science blown away
So easily. If Science has expelled
    Diana, naiad, elfin spirits old,
Still, are not deeper mysteries upheld
    And multitudes of poems left untold?
Reviled Science has wonders of her own:
    Mitochondria, dilated time,
All chemists synthesizing acetone
    Shape, in crucibles, new paradigms.
And chaos, amid shifting eigenstates
And strange attractors, transubstantiates.

Editor's Note: *For the convenience of readers, and in the tradition of publishers who include links to specific original works when publishing a modern poetic response, here is Poe's original sonnet, which is now in the public domain.*

    Sonnet—To Science • *Edgar Allan Poe*
Science! true daughter of Old Time thou art!
    Who alterest all things with thy peering eyes.
Why preyest thou thus upon the poet's heart,
    Vulture, whose wings are dull realities?
How should he love thee? or how deem thee wise,
    Who wouldst not leave him in his wandering

To seek for treasure in the jeweled skies,
    Albeit he soared with an undaunted wing?
Hast thou not dragged Diana from her car?
    And driven the Hamadryad from the wood
To seek a shelter in some happier star?
    Hast thou not torn the Naiad from her flood,
The Elfin from the green grass, and from me
The summer dream beneath the tamarind tree?

Vanity
Juan Manuel Perez

Reflecting off the slicing, shiny blade
A lasting beautiful image of me
A lovely, screaming portrait of me
An enduring, haunting memory of me
Death be so kind, unblind
Dying with a sparkling smile
So that crime-scene snapshots
Permeate my photogenicy
Explaining not who did me wrong
But about how good I look dead

Lion Heart
Tim Pratt

I settle for the first
oracle I can find (there's
no sense being picky in
a situation like mine),
a spirit bound by
old bubblegum and lost coins
in the vicinity of a local
playground.

Crouching in the tawny sand
beneath a scuffed red slide at dawn
I sift the grains between
my fingers until a structure
spontaneously forms: less sand
castle than sand temple, sand
ziggurat, sand tower
of silence. A shape

moves within, a flutter of
shadow in the miniature oval windows,

dweller from some deep desert structure,
denizen of an emptier quarter,
transported to this park at the corner
of two long and aimless streets.

A voice of rippling oasis
water whispers the word "Offerings," and
I empty the contents of a plastic bag on
the ground: a blue pacifier shaped
like a butterfly, the last drops of mother's
milk retrieved from a bottle in the back
of the freezer, a lock of curled hair

yellow

as desert sun, bound by
thread and fraying into strands.

"Ask," the voice whispers,
and I say—I speak—I sigh—
"Should I try
again?"

The ziggurat collapses into a mound,
covering my offerings, and my fallen
hopes fall further still. But then a green
shoot squirms up from the sand and bows
under the sudden blossom
of a yellow flower.

The laughter of absent children flutters
through the empty park. And for the first
time in months, the lion's jaws
locked
around my heart
ease their grasp.

The Magic Walnut
Sofía Rhei; translated by Lawrence Schimel

On slaying the boar, he found an intact walnut
inside its mouth: the beast's teeth had not been able
to even scratch it. He tried to open the nut
with all his weapons, without success. He brought
the dead boar home and gave the nut to his little daughter
to play with. The little girl, without a single word, placed
the animal's soul between its teeth again, and the beast
got to its feet and ran from there.

Ravel: An Etymology
Matthew Richards

The verb *ravel* dates back to the 1580s.
It means "to tangle." To become confused.
It also means "to untangle." "To unravel."
To unwind yourself like a ball of yarn rolling
off the couch and across the kitchen rug.

The contradiction originates in the
Dutch practices of weaving and sewing.
When a thread frays, it ravels, creating
knots too tight to be undone.

My Mémère was a seamstress.
She worked as a finish-stitcher for J. F. McElwain,
making hundreds of shoes every day.

At 91, she became a defunct
sewing machine. Raveled back to her childhood.
Tried to collect the tattered threads of her language.

The doctor said she had knots in her brain.

Do you remember third grade, the Chinese
finger trap that wouldn't let go no matter how
hard you tugged? Do you remember the metal
of your parents' car when it folded into
itself on the highway? Or the ficus outside
your window that strangled the maple tree?

Do you remember your daughter's smile
before you left for work this morning?
How did the teeth of the VCR look when
it ate her favorite movie for breakfast?

One day, you will emerge from your loom,
a crippled silkworm stumbling towards
wholeness. You will not realize that you've
spun yourself a web. That your body knows
parts of itself it couldn't have named.

There is no core to this sickness.
You have all the thread you need.

The Physics Major Agrees to Take the English Major Stargazing
Andrew Rihn

Triangulation is its own form of peer review,
she says to me, absentmindedly,
except we call it parallax.
In my field, we call it subject position
or point-of-view: as good a reason as any
to doubt the existence of an objective reality.
I place the palm of my hand over my right eye,
then my left. The world steps to the side,
as if making way. Objects closest to me
adjust the most. The right eye doesn't know
what the left eye is seeing, but somewhere
in this skull of mine the images merge.
In my field, we call this *revision*.
The stars don't seem to change at this distance.
She goes on to explain the largest parallax
we have is the earth's orbit. *Imagine
the patience it takes to wait six months
between measurements.* Imagine the differences
between what she sees and what I see.
Imagine the distance between our two bodies.

The Seas of Time
Ty Russell

As a girl I predicted
my first rainstorm
      then stood in the barn
and pointed
to where my father
      would die
Child, he said
      His eyes were terrified

Years later I dropped
a plate from the dinner table
      and remembered it
           happening in a dream
The pieces fell like marbles
into designated holes
      as if the plate had always been broken
      always been shards that I had chosen
not to reassemble

I am a sailor

swimming the seas of time
        untethered and so aware
            of depth but not of distance to the shore
Soon I will have a daughter
whom I will mourn
        from the moment of her birth

Oh what I would give
        to not know this much

Luna Satyricon
R. Paul Sardanas and Tisha Garcia

Men who say the moon is cold
are astray, sadly lost in the visions
of fallow winter and hard silver shadows
that dissect the night.
Women know better than this,
and when a cool caress of milky light
touches breast, rests on forehead,
then sons who do not know
the daughter, mother, and crone
have embraced dust at the cost of lifeblood.
Woman, body awash
with tides that the moon can touch
and chants that can reach above
the ring of sky where she rides.
Shall I finally kiss you in all places
under Luna's benediction?
Your feet, scented like the fine sands
they have walked;
knees that will soon bend
when you kneel.
Womb of secret heat,
its taste the deepest exhalation of the soul's want.
It will make a man mad, make a man sane.
To take each breast in my mouth,
Priest to Priestess, right to left,
will render me rippling water,
to reach your lips, to pour in,
finding the deep quenching sea of your lust.
Men who knew little of ecstasy
still knew enough to call the moon a goddess,
an echo, at least, of what once filled them
when they could lie foot to foot
with a woman who knew the moon.
Then, wand and rose were sacred words,

key and lock to the drinking
of white passion in dream,
and love that merits the word.
Love softly under her gaze,
love wildly in her light.
Her light is ours, life calls to life,
exalted brilliance, given flesh.

the more space
Ann K. Schwader

the more space
the fewer stars
left to us
counting again tonight
I find one missing

Past Human
Ann K. Schwader

All men are created equal but we
can fix that now:
                     elixir genes
for our rewired/reloaded minds,
the pristine ping of clockwork hearts
with crystal chips & atom beats,
a nudge to certain balky glands.

All men are defeated equal yet we
fixate on more:
                  some fivescore years
at least before our dread of dark,
a labyrinth of diagrams
denying merely mutant change,
the weight of tech against Thoth's scale.

All men are repeated equal till we
stand fixed as this:
                    a tribe of one
beneath its polished mirror moon,
bereft of stars & flesh & all
unshaped unbidden miracles,
these aliens we made ourselves.

Lanterns
Alexandra Seidel

Once Halloween
was carved out of a pumpkin
Once Halloween
was said to raise the souls of Earth's dead
but no more; nobody remembers
what a pumpkin was or felt or looked like
we instead carve masks from metal
and make our lanterns of discarded diodes

We do not need many lanterns here
to raise the dead
because the dead are few
compared to the million generations
Earth withered in her clutches

Or perhaps
Earth's lost souls traveled with us through space
hungry for our warmth
and lonely without our prayers

Or
they came with us
because we were the jack-o'-lanterns
the candle wicks [or
wicked candles] burning
past things away
and illuminating the hollow faces
our spaceships scratched into the dark

slit sea cucumber
John W. Sexton

slit sea cucumber
bleeds dreams of light . . . a knife
photographs the moon

The Human Guest
Marge Simon

The mating time was brief this year.
Our women sang notes like
floss on the widewind plains.

A human came who forced his seed
on Ala of the Yellow Eyes. We pretended
to be honored; we felt otherwise.

After, Ala wasn't the same.
She cut her marvelous hair,
which had been dark and long,
grown down below her legs.

She wandered off to the Darklands,
heavy with child and none to celebrate.
We mourn her fate. If she survives,
she'll raise his spawn alone.

She was the envy of us all.
When the child is born,
she'll burn his father's image
in the sands of our dead oceans.

The human sits on our sacred stones.
He preens his beard and leers at females,
with no more thoughts to waste on Ala;
he never even knew her name.

Come burrow season, we prepare,
sharpen our talons on caddo root.
When the freezing gales begin,
the human will demand sanctuary,
as his kind always does.

We will confirm his welcome
with the strewing of his bones.

Visitors
Marge Simon

I'd steal outside at night, hoping for
a sign of contact, something from those
on that parallel line I knew were there.

Arms around my legs, I'd sit
for hours under the cold stars until
the mountain air drove me inside.

I graduated, left those early fantasies behind.

Then one day at a boutique, while

trying on a certain hat, they called,
though none could hear.

I bought it and I wear it well,
a shield against the conflicts,
the jealousies and fears, the lies—
there's another world beside our own.
I believe they know we're here.

The Elusive Language of Purple Birds
Robin Spriggs

He wanted, more than anything, to understand. So in his last few moments, before his heart fell still and his brain went black, he called upon the birds that had often visited him in dreams, the little purple birds with beaks of orange peel and eyes like his grandmother's; he called upon them in a make-believe version of the language they had taught him in his sleep, the mysterious, elusive language he had always forgotten immediately upon waking, the language that, even now, he could only counterfeit; but as he called out, pretending with all his might, he realized that his mouth—like those of the purple birds—had become a beak of orange peel, and he could taste the orange on his tongue, the orange of youth and summer and the awful ache of becoming, and the taste reminded him of that day so long ago when he had seen a certain girl at the park, a girl in a crowd, a girl about his own age, a girl who had seen him too, but only for an instant, only in passing, seen him and smiled a smile like the birth of a brand-new universe, so bright and painfully beautiful it transfixed him where he stood, froze him in his tracks on the brink of a timid "Hello," and there he remained while the people and the dogs and the days came and went, came and went, and during that time he neither ate nor drank nor moved, but the girl's smile—tickling, torturing—had taken root in his heart, and on this alone did he subsist, until one day (a week or a month or perhaps a year later) he was able to move again, to move and eat and drink, and to go forth into this newborn universe to find the girl who had made him a stranger to his former, lesser self; but find her he never did, despite a lifetime of trying, though along the way he had found many *other* things, many other lovely things—found them and lost them and sometimes (when lucky) found them to lose them again, and by and by, much to his despair, even his recollection of the girl began to fray at the edges, to blur in the middle, and to fade from hither to yon, but her smile remained in his heart all the days of his life, promising a promise that—because he lacked the words—he could never claim as his own, yet suddenly, now, well-nigh the end of this final ragged breath, the words (the birds!), the elusive, inscrutable words—violet-feathered, orange-peel-beaked, and, yes, grandmother-eyed—descend from the sky in a purple song of passage, to wrap him in a shroud of winged understanding and bear him away to a heaven of his own peculiar design, where the price of admission is a spoken-for promise and a smile at long last returned.

Grendel's Mother
Heidy Steidlmayer

When the moon's worn scutcheon
touches the flint-gray flood,
I will lave him in foxglove
and vetch until the blood
of his wretched heart heals.

Without a scar, he stood—

as the men make their way
into the quaking wood.

idiointerventionist (or, "but I interrupt myself")
W. Gregory Stewart

Some years ago (and without mentioning it),
                      my inner child
took an after-school job
as the monster under my bed.

Now, I've known about this since at least the 7th grade but
                      nevertheless kept my mouth shut in the interest
                      of intrapersonal peace,
until I recently found out
that my imaginary best friend
                also knew—all this time—
and said *nothing*.

Of course
                a blow up amongst me
                is inevitable . . .
I just haven't decided how to broach the inner dialog,

but *some*time soon,
                one of me
will be coming out of
                some kind of closet,
                *some*where,
but really, by this point I am not even mildly curious about
                who will get custody
                of whom
when I finally do.

                I'm just looking forward to the fight.

Dead Hotels
Anna Sykora

In our ignorance
We booked a tour to a war zone,
Paradise before Yugoslavia's demise,
And there on the south Dalmatian coast
Lay several dead hotels.

One splayed on a hill above the wrinkled sea;
Trees burst from the roofless bungalows
And green vines cascaded from gaping windows:
Grapevines and ivy, glossy-leaved.
Geraniums had leaped from the broken terra-cotta,
Reception down the hill now just a slab
Of cracked cement and diligent ant hills.

We stayed in a kitchen with new rooms,
Where skinny locals feasted with their lovers
On Sunday's all-you-can-eat buffet,
Bitter at the years their wars devoured:
We will never catch up with our past.

Nearby we found salt-tasty figs,
And a second hotel picked clean as a shell;
Skull-marked bottles tethered near the dock,
Condoms bobbing gently beside them,
Warned of unexploded ordnance.

Down the road stood a lonely house,
Windows scorch-marked, shutters torn away
And lean inhabitants eyeing us with fear:
Why were we staring at this house?
What were we wanting here?

A rest, we'd thought
In our ignorance.
Where armies stormed in and broke, burned and looted,
Where the blue sea rippled like a grimace,
We thought we'd sun ourselves and leave.

Taking the Auspices
Sonya Taaffe
(for Erik Amundsen)

The language I know best
blows under the shadows of pines,

turns from the bones of green branches
like the small bells hanged in my hair.
Look, I have a knife's edge
to the cold bark, my warm hand
at your throat. I have a god's name
at the edges of my mouth.
The moon is silent when she turns this color,
softer than the rotten blood of a heart.

Red Grown
James E. Tolan

He doesn't recognize her
without her cloak and blush,

though she cannot forget
who first treated her like food.

His smile, when she takes him
to her cottage in the woods,

perhaps he wishes it
were tender, hopes she will be

a taste of heaven in the flesh,
a spring lamb born to slaughter,

but, as soon as he paws
her ruddy belt, she will carve

across his gullet a smile
more sincere, then roll him

from her bed, his furry carcass
limp and fat as a belly full

of undigested grandmother.

Graffiti Tree
Mary Turzillo

A thousand years ago
before defeat of gravity
you carved our names
on the graffiti tree,

not knowing it would grow

through stratosphere,
through shimmering auroras,
twisting, resisting torque
of low, then high earth orbit,

unpocked by passing satellites,
while our initials climbed,
imbedded in its bark
as scars (and promises) do:

tallest tree ever,
reaching for that milky light,
the full moon,

and when it found
the Mare Imbrium,
it gently brushed that dust,
slowing the moon's turning incrementally

until all lovers on the earth,
and on the moon too,
asked, oh, who were they,
those two who carved a bridge
between two worlds?

Moving to Enceladus
Mary Turzillo
(for Shirley)

My dear Shirley,
now that we are moving to Enceladus,
I regret that we never visited
the Victorian Perambulator Museum in Jefferson, Ohio,
nor the Tuba Hall of Fame in Okemos, Michigan.

I'm leaving behind my tapes of *Chicken Soup for the Undead Soul*,
which you may use for your convenience,
or donate
to the Society for Photosynthesizing Cats.

Remember in my absence
the extreme whiteness of that one Saturnian moon
and how an entire collection
of action figures from the musical of *Titus Andronicus*
can go missing if you don't watch the fissures
in our own neighbor planet's ice cap.

I will write to you

and a special automaton with catlike whiskers
will jump-kick my electrons
(embedded in Death's Head orchid petals)
all the way to your pillow.

I apologize for mentioning death, Shirley,
since you have inadvertently forgotten to remain alive,
and as the last and most whimsical of your race
have abandoned me to my petty vices and downbeat thrift.

I am not done with weeping of course.
There is only one leave-taking, and I do it every time
any moon
anywhere
rises in any sky.

To the ancients, the sea was a dangerous place
Anna Waite

To the ancients, the sea was a dangerous place
Full of great monsters; the kraken, the whale.
As he bent to the struggle with oar and sail,
A sailor often begged Poseidon for grace.
How pleasant it was to see a familiar face!
The playful seal that chased away fear,
Clowning about where the shore was near,
And crowning each rock with a sprawling brace.

But the sailor that smiled at sight of a seal
Oft changed his mind when he returned home.
For the wife he thought of with each empty night
Had been charmed away by the same playful zeal
And kisses that tasted of the ocean's foam.
O selkie, you stole our sailor's delight!

The Kite
Kyla Lee Ward

She goes home tonight.
By day she mourns like a wet nurse,
giving her tears to those not her own.
She walks in procession through the necropolis,
beating her breast and tearing her hair;
good figure, long hair, and she never stints.
The troupe leader favors her. She always
shares the funeral meal and coin.

But tonight, as torches cluster at the gate
like the bright clouds cluster in the west, she goes home.
Not to the city of the living,
but back into the silent clutter of tombs.
This place is old. The watchmen keep
to the paved roads and crypts with names.
But centuries pass as she walks uphill,
treading shards of sculpture, fragments of stone
and bronze. No lights here, no offerings;
such things attract worse than dogs.
That's why she broke the seals after the funeral,
to keep him safe. She remembers that day:
yellow is the color of funerals,
of sunlight, disease, and the flesh of women.
Now the sky is indigo and wind creeps chill
through a door that she opened, inch by inch,
to a crypt whose first owner had been erased,
barely large enough to contain his outer shell.
Not a good likeness: no likeness at all.
The symbol of a man. They placed it here
and left him. It took her weeks to work the lid aside.
Now her hands sink into linen ripped asunder.
A robber, seeing this, will dig no more,
but he still lies just as he did
when the priest anointed the eyes and mouth
of his mask. A likeness there;
the faintest identity in red and black.
Then they drew the shroud across.
No house since then, no name; for there was
no child and his brother didn't want her.
She did not want him. She was a child herself
when they married. But she knew love.
Red is for the flesh of men. Through bandages,
at last she touches; her feet slip through the crack.
Sinking through shrouds and shawls, the scent
of spices replaced by resin.
Her body measures his.
Her hand explores the coldness of his chest.
Cheek to a shoulder hard and slick
as a carved pillow. Deep in the linen of their bed
she rests. Beside him she can sleep.

A Greater Moon
Gerald Warfield

In the end, a final breath.
No sight or sound, I think,

but the universe contained
within a single ebb and flow.

That breath,
totem of a greater tide,
joins its kin within
a single cosmic sigh.

For each life, one season,
and from its farthest ebb, no return.
No call of moon nor sun nor stars may rouse it,
singly, from its last retreat.

Yet upon the sea there are many tides,
and on the tides many waves
in turn that rise and fall and
clamor to be heard and not to die.

I am told
of a universe that expands,
and of a last retreat
from which there is no escape.

But perhaps the breath of life, once drawn,
does not exhaust itself
but joins again a greater tide,
summoned by a greater moon.

A wave, once dashed upon the strand,
does not rise and fall again.
Yet join it must the tide that brought it thus
to end upon unyielding shores.

The universe expands;
the universe contracts.
Who is to say it is not called
by a greater moon
that summons tides on endless shores
where endless waves exhaust themselves
though singly rise no more.

Escaping the Dawn
Jacqueline West

Their hunger builds in the last hours.
Streetlamps flicker, the small storms
of moths and mayflies long departed.
Gradual as a freeze, the liquid dark

turns white, ice trapping the moment
in anesthesia. Stars dull their corners.
The moon dissolves, a brittle skull
swirled to the edge of a seashell.
This is their warning. Dragged back
into closets, to the dust under beds,
to dark corners, to graffiti-spattered
holes, they mutter, unsatisfied, licking
their fingers. Day takes its first breath
on the horizon as they stagger slowly
back toward the darkness, always just
out of reach of those long, bright hands.

A Modest Suggestion
Neal Wilgus

The Rhysling Awards for the best science fiction, fantasy, and horror poetry are given annually by the Science Fiction Poetry Association. Named for "Noisy" Rhysling, the blind poet in Robert Heinlein's story "The Green Hills of Earth," the awards are divided into two categories—short poems (1-49 lines) and long poems (50+ lines). Recently the SFPA added the Dwarf Stars Award for speculative poems of ten lines and under.

I would like to take this trend even further and suggest the Black Hole Award for speculative poems with no lines at all. Here are a few samples:

> Black Hole Speaks
> —NW

> One Hand Clapping
> —NW

> Absolute Zero
> —NW

> Zero Gravity
> —NW

> Don't Go There
> —NW

> Whatever
> —NW

> ?
> —NW

Finally, I would suggest the Big Bang Award for speculative poems with an infinite number of lines—but of course such poems would take forever to read!

Angel's Den
Stephen M. Wilson

The golden-green
scales of seraph wings
glisten in the nebulous
depths of the angel's
den

a lamina blanketing
centuries of grizzled
bones sucked dry of their
marrow and the fresh rot of
carrion corpses.

A familiar fetor of fear
emanates from the
new quarry,
exciting Gabriel
to erection.

Shimmers of a lurid grin
expose barbed teeth,
which he sinks into the
tender white belly
of the child.

Christogenesis
Stephen M. Wilson

Pale Horse wins the Kentucky Derby as minute red angels dance on
                                                                              pristine
                                                                              retinas.
        Surrounded . . .
        Surrounded!
I alone, in the cafe of dreams, await
Quetzalcoatl's second coming—a myriad of pyramids sprout from liquid
asphalt walls mocking the bloody cinnamon froth of my cacao pod latte.
        tzolkin deciphers the
        Ternary Code   1 2 2 1 2 0 1 2
              of my infection. Pale Man *has* returned! Conquistador/I *am*
Pale—a singularity (avatar or jockey?)
I AM One Hunahpu, come out of the alligator's mouth!
I am risen!
Arms outstretched, feet unshod, I travel the *Xibalba be* . . .

```
                o       u
         r              n
    r                       d
         u      alone
                        e
  s
                d

                Mother
                was right.
```

Closure
Greer Woodward

For her third and final wish,
she asked the genie
to seal her conscience
in the vacant lamp
and toss it in the sea—
a wise precaution,
given her first two wishes.

LONG POEMS FIRST PUBLISHED IN 2011

The King of Cats, the Queen of Wolves
Mike Allen, Sonya Taaffe, and Nicole Kornher-Stace

1.
These gouges where glaciers furrowed toward the sea
were smooth-sloped still, ice-muscled, snowbound;
these waves, a salt-waste of frozen crests: and we
were handprints of smoke on ochre walls, the ghosts
of birds in dying flutes, the first time (they say)
the king of cats and the queen of wolves clashed.

Time had no current, lay still in all directions.
Gods and beasts and beast-gods stalked
each other across star-hot sand, through
tree-high grass, into forests that swathed
continents, where dragons long as rivers
shimmered through the branches, beneath
nights deep as the teeming abyss of Sea.
He walked alone across tundra oceans,
danced deadly through infinite verdant canopies;
she ghosted the ground beneath, golden eyes
seeking from shadow, a glint of silver and sable
in primeval snow. Her children huddled always
beneath her cloak, still without voice or form;
he had no followers, but the strength of a host.

Charcoal crumbled across a cavern's ribs. Limestone
stained with torchlight, smoothed with time. Here
his eyes glint blackly, and there her tracks mark
north, truer than iron; but meteors fell and blazed
like untold angels as her teeth raked his throat,
his claws set in her shoulders, and here red ochre
smears for their blood that glittered (they say)
into garnet where it fell. How she tore her mouth
free to scream down the moon, how the tides
bulged and spilled over at her tempestuous howl;
how his strength rippled as he dragged the earth
aside, one hooked and contemptuous shrug,
and the delta lay differently then. Ice-floes
into warm swamps, magma cracking upward
beneath chill plains, sand skidded into snow
and all the globe torn awry in their battle:
all the nameless powers of beforetime rapt
to see whose children would inherit the earth.

Salt of blood and salt of ocean were one,
libations of violence that drenched day into night.
The might of their convulsions subsided, as must
all aftershocks; the outcome of their intimate war
undecided: each had torn the other countless ways,
subdivided selves roaming broken terrains, tundras
wrenched from jungles, peaks ripped from plains.
The battle neither won nor lost: momentum fractalled
in infinite directions, unfocused by entropy;
only the children, single cells of once great gods
remained, things of claws, teeth, stalking, silence,
united in death and hunger and hatred.

Time, punctured in fury, began its flow.

2.
The hall bustles with finery; to gaze
upon such silk and lace, white fur and blood-
red sashes, ribbons twined in wigs, a dance
of noble plumage, is to know that time
is just a toy to each pale-powdered face,
a strange place to resume epochs-old hunt;

yet silent blows the horn that starts the hunt
when, stepping to the flute, her wary gaze,
so vulpine-sharp, alights upon his face,
its supple bones, a smile that could draw blood;
a raging echo from the birth of time
commands them both, and as they close to dance,

their spirits have entwined unseen and dance
quite differently through half-remembered hunt,
claws and teeth that tore at flesh and time
a whirlwind through their minds as they gaze
into each other's eyes, a taste of blood
tinting both their tongues as they face

each well-remembered, unfamiliar face
that paces in this politesse. This dance
traced to a pattern deeper still than blood
or bone that yet might falter in the hunt—
if minuets have tamed her moon-burned gaze
to shadowplay, worn token over time,

or if, within this masquerade of time,
he has misplaced his lover's, killer's face—
but watch how sleekly he bows to her gaze
and how her fingers vise his in the dance

as though his skin might slip. Now for the hunt
that reckons its spoils in more ways than blood;

a breath passed back and forth, the beat of blood
that faster than their measured steps keeps time
to the race of hearts, tuned to her hunter's
silence mirrored in his lean-eyed face
as finally he pulls her close to dance
beneath the hall's incurious, ageless gaze.

Her lip-rouge stained like blood upon his face,
where for a time he trapped her in his dance—
the hunt releases them to their shared gaze.

> Perhaps in an unfathomable design
> woven tight as atoms, deeper than sea,
> fabric firmed before ruptured time's flow,
> all odds of enmity require this chance:
> two things born from hate will meet and love,
> and spin the clay of fear into new shapes.
>
> In the dark their shadows form one shape
> that etches strange calligraphy, a sign
> announcing the unknown, new forms of love
> born in a humble chamber; do they see,
> the courtesans dancing below? What chance
> have they to sense the tremors flow
>
> through time's thin web, as lovers flow
> against each other, pressing savage shapes
> onto startled skin; without a chance
> to understand the shiver in the air, this sign
> of shattering change, the heedless dancers see
> to their steps with masked facades of love
>
> pressed cheek to cheek; how we all love
> to hook limbs in bestial pairings and flow
> in practiced mimicry of rites born in the sea
> and before, when a mate or killer took shape
> in the dark and a partner awaited the sign
> to join or flee. As below, so above, a chance
>
> meeting of godsparks leaves the world no chance
> to spin unchanged; their furor masked as love
> bent on mutual destructions, all the signs
> clawed in their skin, in teeth marks that flow,
> in the taste of each other's blood, shapes
> their bodies form, echoes of that struggle seen

before time began. At the height do they see
these fragments embedded within? Is there chance
for them to glimpse these primal shapes,
the Queen astonished in the power of her love's
embrace, the startled King's arch and flow—
Fate's tapestry restitched in new design.

Seeking meaning in this unexpected love,
at first chance she asks scrying water's flow
what shape the child will take, but gleans no sign.

3.
From the pierced heart of the world, time gouts
and stutters, gouts and trickles to surcease. The hall
is wrack, cold carrion beneath a sunless noon, spoils
of no war but entropy. So too the other battlefields
and bridebeds have flared and dimmed, each one a pan-flash
in a plate of ice, each imprinted with its sullen,
crimson ghost. She stalks what once were roads. Moons
pare themselves to nothing and ripen anew, rearing
through a pall of ash; neither her cat's eyes nor
her wolf's nose deign to crave that feeble light. She walks:
as one, the ghosts of ghosts, pale hunting-trophies
on time's bloodied belt, will turn to her, then cringe away—
and each one wears her face. At her footfall, holographic flowers
flicker out.

It was not always thus. Her hunt was once a hunt; the city once
a city, or a ruined city, or a meadow where a ruined city stood.
Now there are walls, or ghosts of walls, or ivy clutched
to nothing where the ghosts of walls once loomed: no fire
rains down around her; no wolf's-claw, cat's-claw banners raised
where she had thought to sleep (though their holograms, archived
in the city's histories, do flicker in and out betimes, in quick
succession, or else overlaid, one veining through the other like
a leaf held to the sun). Her mother's bloodline
and her father's both reach back and back through time, hand over
hand, as though drawing pails up from dry wells—but never
forward, and none remain to tell her her own secrets. She camps
the murals 'til they round their circuit, flicker in: she sees the cities
rise, the feline and the lupine both; she sees the walls forget
who raised them; she sees each one's inhabitants go interloping
through the other's gates; she sees wars, détentes, truces
sublimated into legend as the bombs wail down—truces forged anew
upon the finding of a common enemy: the spreading web of by-blows
with hearts that pump the blood of both. Now they are dust, her mother's
kin, her father's; she alone slogs on, despite their greatest efforts
unannihilated, though the shots still dog her dreams, and she wakes

ducking, rolling, baring claws her grandam's grandam might
have worn, which every time resolve to fingertips, soft and unavailing,
in the light.

They say (they *said*, for who remains to say?)
the king of cats, the queen of wolves died childless,
were each reborn, and childless died again: each iteration torn
from his/her father's/mother's side, a tumor whose metastasis
gnawed worlds to dust, sucked stars like eggs, raked time's weft
shrieking out of true. Thronged by ghosts of her past selves she hunts,
each feinting as she feints, each pouncing at the shadow of the one before,
each empty-handed, empty-clawed, clean-toothed and parched
for blood. By her cat's-heart's, wolf's-heart's metronome she walks,
the last in line, the shadowless, unmoored in time, and trusting to
her mother's strength, her father's luck: when at last a shadow
turns to her unbidden, eyes glazed with lust for blood or flesh,
her muscle memory will give reply; when at last time wakes from stasis,
shakes her clinging from its crippled back, regardless for how long,
how far she falls, she will land always, always
on her feet.

Desfixion
Erik Amundsen

In prime and in chief I call you my siblings,
we who suckled together at the kindness of our mother,
we who sucked and grew fat on her bounty,
fat, and also strong. Hers are the tusks that rend,
hers is the mouth that trails the gut in red ropy streamers,
her claws are those wet with the lives of the foolish and vain.
Listen, in prime and in chief,
you who tasted of her milk, to the cry of our father.
His breath is the killing blast of the winter;
his heart is the rage of ten thousand furnaces;
his belly is full of the lightning of all storms. Know him,
know him, and listen.
I've seen an army of children formed;
I've seen an army of child hands forced to hold,
forced to give honor and praise, trained, not well,
given swords, given a vision of a heaven, a sky
they won't ever see, nor anyone who brings their given piece
their given piece of metal down.
I call, I cry, and hear me, in prime, listen, in chief,
and raise a voice with me, be it the howl of the pack
of the hungriest wolves or be it the hiss of the basket
that holds the serpents. I will take them.
I will take the number, from first to none, with open hand,

slap those weapons to the ground, and those children,
yes, they'll know my hand, they'll feel my palm,
but their leaders, the ones who made the metal,
the ones who, like a father, bent those little fingers
around the hilt and pommel, those men, they will know
my venom, tooth and nail. In chief, they will learn.
In prime, they must be made to know.
A mother bore each child in that rout; a father should
have taught them how to hold themselves, as ours did.
Their leaders, in chief, create a hell, light its fire;
they must learn, in prime, should they seek
to send their children down to fire,
let it be them who come to know the fire.
They who send their children to the mouth of the glutton,
they know nothing of the belly of Moloch.
It is time that they came to understand.
It is time for them to learn.

This is your moment, balanced,
a stood-up, jagged piece of glass,
and in a moment, a weapon.

> In second and to my sight I call you, my adversaries;
> I see you are in numbers and by those numbers
> I am bound, with left hand scalded by fires,
> right hand run with chilblains; you I will sort
> as though I sorted apples in two baskets.
> To my sight I see you, adversaries, you men,
> you women of other lands and times, and a war
> that stands between us. War, but without hate,
> I break the head off of that spear, I crush it out
> and grind the head into the earth and leave it,
> as a serpent to be taken by the scavenging bird.
> You see me, in second, now, without my paint,
> no plume, no armor, just my flesh, I come, as you
> came, to my sight, in second, I offer a hand,
> and you may strike it, but you must also take it up.
> This has gone too long; in my sight,
> I see the field piled with us, our coring,
> our peels, and the vinegar stink of us.
> If you say the dead tell us to fight,
> I say you know nothing of the dead, and it's time
> for you to see them for yourself.
> Look into my eye; this is not violence, this is truth.
> In second, in my sight, I see the other,
> my adversaries through failure, through betrayal,
> those who were given to rule, but let the crown
> slip over their eyes; those given to plenty,

who left my siblings in hunger and want;
those given to spirit and chose a spirit of hate;
those given to strength who picked up that spear,
the one now broken, the one now ground out
in second, as it should have been in prime,
as it never should have been at all.
You profit from this no more. I have spoken
to the bees, and they will deny you their sweet;
I have spoken to the hornets, and to the wasps;
I have spoken to the thorns and now, now
they are thirsty, and the stings will drive you there,
from my sight. Your war is broken,
your power, stolen in second, stolen, squandered
spent. You gave blood to Gods of War, and now
they are drunk and will not listen when you cry,
and in my sight, you will be as washing,
wind-torn from the line, scattered in the thorns,
pierced, and in the sun, in a second, will you dry.
The butcher birds will pierce their meals
on the thorns of your resting place.
No one else will know where you have gone.

    Everything is relative in this dark land,
    this flattened plain, vastness ahead,
    fastness behind, and there are thorns
    and voices caught, voices tattered.
Everything is relative in this dark land;
this is not smoke or cloud, it is black,
against a black sky; it has no smell,
but sound. I saw it turn and thunder
toward me in the shape of horses
with lightning for eyes, lightning
the color of salmon flesh, I saw
this—what remained when the tower fell
and the sky cleared.
Everything is relative in this dark land;
these are stars that circle our sky,
but they are not our stars. This refrain,
this is the breath between two screams;
this is the rage when it comes in.
Everything is relative in this dark land;
to know your sins, name them, to name
your sins, you must own them;
the devil was weak and cold
lying in the desert, so I picked him up,
he was my devil, and now, now
he is still my devil, I might never be his,

never again, but our sins, we share,
we share them all in common,
and everything is relative in this dark land.

    This is the end, as the tower falls;
    the smoke will clear,
    lights in the skies we took as stars
    reveal themselves as Gods.

    In final and in closing I call you unnamed, you
    invisible, voiceless, those lost in the sea,
    lost in the echo that transmits in soundless space,
    you yet to be, children and dead, unbegotten.
    The wind will press down upon the fields
    and the grasses sway, and the things come down;
    we have no name; they are great, like clouds,
    terrible like storms, and their justice is terrible
    in closing. Calamity, catastrophe, the bad star,
    now fallen, will gather the evil that brought it up,
    gather as fish at the weirs, caught, gasping,
    in final. I call nothing to crash in where something
    had been wrong; the surgeon heals
    in closing the wound made by the surgeon's hand.
    All the things that have been taken and lost,
    all those in final places, those names not remembered,
    those faces never again seen, they gather,
    and in closing, they witness. Witness this,
    I cry out, in final, the place where stones only listen.
    Before the final leaf falls to the ground,
    before the conflict grows so foolish that the world,
    that the people die of shame, closing up the book
    of this world, these lives, with more than half
    of its pages blank. These stars are not our stars,
    this world is not our world to destroy,
    and from suicide, in final, are we forbidden.
    This is my curse unto you: you who would be the last,
    you who would burn the world for a moment alone
    with a destruction you call God, I curse you to live,
    live and regret. Live and feel shame, and be known,
    be known by the unknown for the things you have done,
    those who have no voice and no sight, I call you,
    use my eyes, use my mouth, speak with me.
    Life, then, it is for you all to live in the shapes
    of the scorn of all of us, you fools, you conquerors,
    you would-be destroyers. You will bleed a river,
    bleed your own blood, enough to fill the ocean,
    and never do your veins run dry; you are despicable,
    and you will live to be despised. Calamity.
    Catastrophe. In final and in closing, I curse you

with inconsequence. The world taken from you,
the world like a toy, that you, spoiled child, made
of it, in closing and in final, once and for all.
We make a place for you among the friendless,
and though I am filthy as well, you who profit,
you will be known as filthier still. My hate dies
as you live, as your dreams are yanked,
like the reins of the cart from the driver, a fool,
and passed into the hands of those whose faces
you have forgotten and condemned to invisibility;
they will rule your fate for now, in final, in closing,
in this world, without an end.

So be it.

The Curator Speaks in the Department of Dead Languages
Megan Arkenberg

Every year, there are people—not many,
but some—who send me charcoal rubbings,
etchings, transcriptions from old tombs
and ask me what they mean.
Some, I can translate; we reached
the language in time, or the phrase survives
idiomatically in other tongues,
or guesswork is enough to patch
the ragged edges of what we know.
But every year, there are some I cannot find,
some I cannot save.

Why do I hate it so much, writing
these letters, these terse apologies for failing
to satisfy a stranger's curiosity? That's all
it is; these tombs do not belong to
parents, old lovers, or even more distant relations.
Most have stood silent for centuries.
Yet there are people who care enough
to ask what they said, and I must admit
guilty ignorance.

When I was a very small girl,
I found a broken chickadee beneath
the oak that held its nest. I took it in,
washed it and fed it rice and built it
a nest of soft rags, but it lived only
one night. I cried hard at its death,
as long and hard as I would cry for my mother's

decades later. I think of that sometimes
while writing these letters: the awful risk
of caring for strangers.

We cannot save all of them.
Even the ones that survive have been
broken, lamed, their limbs amputated,
their features mangled past recognition.
Inevitably, some pieces are lost. Words
slip through the cracks; nuances are buried
in pauper's graves.

On the red moon of Tzevet'an,
a thief told me of the fourteen words
men cannot say to women,
but there were no other men
in the ice-bound prison where he died.
The words are lost, unguessable.
The last speaker of the Kao-Kling tongue
was a little girl, four years old, who knew
little more than the names of fruits
and the disease that killed her family.
Her mother had been a flower arranger
to the Lord of Fenkanpao; again and again
the child told me of a flower
as wide as her mother's hand, the blue of fresh milk,
that had the most beautiful name.
She could not remember what it was, and
fever carried her off before
she could show me where it grew.

These are the mysteries
we know about. There are times
my frustration is so great,
my anger at time's merciless entropy
is so strong, that I give voice
to the most punishing thoughts.
How much is buried in the conquered lands,
not only of answers
but of the questions themselves?
How much more plentiful
are the dead without ghosts?

And yet I am trying.
Without funds, without time, sometimes
without love—but I am trying.
If not to save all of them, at least
to leave a marker above the graves.

The Cathedral of the Michaelangelines
Elizabeth Barrette

The full-color brochure flickers
under my fingers, rainbow hues
painting a broad banner:
Picture This! The REAL Artists' Colony!
Two hundred years past landfall
and they're still using their original slogan.

I have to confess, it suits.

The crowd jostles amiably
as I walk toward the day's destination,
the Cathedral of the Michaelangeline Order.
The streets, in places, are paved with real gold.
People rarely try to steal it, considering that
vandalism is a capital crime here, and felons
are sent not to execution but to mines and quarries.
It's an old-fashioned deterrent, but it seems to work.

Buildings rise up on both sides.
Some show flat faces splashed with murals
of galaxies, jungles, gazelopes galloping,
surrealist renderings of giraffes and bathtubs,
people's portraits or kaleidoscopic abstracts.
The rest are architectural marvels
festooned with flying buttresses, columns,
arches and domes, gargoyles and grotesques,
crenellations, fountains, carvings, friezes, frescos.
There is no relief from bas-relief.
A thousand styles tumble together, yet
somehow nothing looks ugly or out-of-place.

At last I come to the cathedral.
Its steeple glistens with silvered glass,
and its rose windows show real rosy quartz
interspersed with ruby and clear crystal.
Seraphim perch over sculptured doorframes.
Inside, the narrow columns and tall candelabras
draw all attention upward.

The ceiling is a marvel—forget
the Sistine Chapel of Old Earth. This
is a masterpiece of technology as well as talent.
Animated stars swirl over the dome,
illustrating the Big Bang before
spiraling into a helix of DNA,
then expanding into animals, humans,

and finally fine arcs of geometric symbols.
My automatic camera follows my eye,
focusing and recording what I see—
which is good, because I've forgotten
all about it, forgotten even about the article
I'm supposed to be researching
for *Galactic Geographic.*

This is how they catch me.
They're priests—they proselytize—
and I'm a professional, so I
paint a smile on my face
and prepare to listen.

God is an Artist,
they declare,
and we can prove it, too.

God loves to create things.
You can see the evidence all around.
He made the universe and filled it
with plants and animals, people and vistas.
How can you look at a woman or a rose,
a prismaticat or a scarlet macaw,
or a nebula nursing infant star systems,
and not conclude that God loves beauty?

Oh, we admit that sometimes
God aims to shock his audience—
but that just proves our point.
He made the lamb and the tiger,
the song-willow and the velocipetal,
the sapphire and the razor-sharp obsidian,
the blue giant and the black hole.

We aren't meant to be ascetics;
We're meant to be artists.
How can we not conclude
that we too are meant to make beauty,
when we are surrounded by
such materials and such models?
Why, it would be a sin to waste them!

We can take a hint.
So we glorify God with art,
creating things as we were created.
We praise Him not with prayer but with paint,
stone and ceramic, metal and wood.

With everything we make, we say:
Be like this. Be beautiful in your soul.

The priests meet my eyes
and repeat that part.
Be beautiful in your soul,
the Michaelangelines urge me.
Be true to the Artist who envisioned you.

Biting my lip, I look again
at the invincible ceiling, call my
hovering camera to my hand, and wonder
if I can do Him justice.

Welcomed Cast Outs
Dana Bell

Blackness.
We came from there.
The dark, dark, whirling center of the galaxy
where stars circle its greedy heart
before they're devoured.

Is it any wonder we're predators?

Pointy ears
which hear what you cannot.
Sharp claws to shred our prey
or maybe your arm, toe, or foot.
The bittersweet taste of blood
our dessert and right.

Yet, you cuddle our furred bodies,
pet our snake-shaped heads,
let us sleep on your shredded couch,
warm chair, and snuggly bed.

Night.
Our time.
So like our ancient home.
Time to hunt and play,
keep you awake
with our games of tag
and pouncing.

Day.
Time to sleep.

Sometimes ask for a pet.
Mostly ignore you.

Or watch the winged things land,
eat,
on metal or wooded houses,
so like your own.

We wish to chase the bushy-tailed ones
who eat the seed and peanuts
you put outside for them
on the white snow
or in the tall green grass.

Grass. The perfect place
for us to wait,
to hunt them.

Instead,
clear glass separates us
from our rightful prey.

Cat TV you tell us.

Yet,
do you not wonder
how we came into your world?

We know the historical records
suggest
it was the storage bins of Egypt
that lured us to you.
After all,
there were hungry rats,
a plentiful food source
for us.

Silly humans.
Not truly how we came into your world.

You see,
the deadly heart
cast us out.
We were too dangerous
and rivaled its power.

There was this portal,
a straw bag

filled with the dust of the desert,
gnawed-on bones,
unfulfilled, lost dreams.

We found it,
entered your realm.
The rightful new hunters
and rulers.

You welcomed us.
Foolish humans.

Gavage
Robert Borski

Small matter that the clipped wings
have grown back; at this stage
in the fattening process the beast
is too big to lift itself off the ground,
let alone fit through the doors
of the royal stable.

Moreover, gelding has further
dociled the beast. As a consequence,
its mouth, scarred from the long-term
placement of the feeding tube, is now
less a flue than a conduit
to the digestive chambers,
while eructation, with or without fire,
is no longer possible.

A good thing for him, thinks
the king's cook, now coming forward
and palpating its hide, mid-shanks.

Oh, my.
The beast's liver is swollen to thrice
its normal size and will almost certainly
be marbled with globules of fat. But
just to be on the safe side, he tells
the soldiers behind him, *One last batch
of forcemeat, laddies.*

More prisoners of war again; but at least
this time it looks as if they have been
given rations recently. Those not rendered
senseless by the forced introduction

to the gullet (the plunger entails the use
of three men and has a lurid rhythm)
can often be heard screaming within,
like animals sack-tossed into a river,
and that is true this time no less
than the last. At least until the gastric
marinade silences all complaints.

Equally so, one learns to ignore
the concentrated stink of scales,
dung, and scraps of old molt. Indeed,
more often than not, thinks the cook,
it helps to concentrate on the overall
mission, perhaps on the finer details
of the recipe, say, or what needs
to be done yet.

Were there not onions still to be picked?
Mace to be ground? Sherry chosen
and butter whipped? Nevertheless,
even before the beast's maroon-
slick lobes can be cut free,
it is hard not to imagine the velvety
iron smoothness of the paté; to not
hear the king's words of praise,
"Good job, cook"; to refrain
in anticipation from licking his lips
over and over and over again,
like a snake sampling the wind.

Surreal Fortune
Bruce Boston

The Horseshoe Spread

Ten of Anvils

Past Influences

Engines of desire
roaming the lost highways
of muscular youth.

An agrestic collage
floating in a fishbowl.

The inversion fields

of an autodidactic summer
obsessed with guitar solos.

The pearl-handled revolver
prominently missing
from the oak mantel.

The Andalusian Dog, Major Arcana 12

Current Situation

The bewildered man
urges the palomino
up a burning slope
despite the handicap
of a thrown shoe.

Beneath a turgid moon
frenzied by outlaw pollen
the wings of a bird
echo in the corridors
of skyscraper dreams.

Traces of the alchemist
are found lingering
in the accidental streets
and forlorn curio bazaars
of a tourist mecca.

The Edwardian Lion, Major Arcana 23, Reversed

Future Avenues

Red veins in a yellow sclera.

A long tale
of the cartographer's
miraculous fountain pen.

Extraordinary fireworks
in fields of feldspar and lace.

Nympholepsy discovered
in a reflective lake.

Proteus, Major Arcana, 9

Courses of Action

Enter with
the sun-shot brilliance
of a polished knife.

Listen to plane crashes
on the acoustic gramophone.

Adjust the rearview mirror
until you see apothegms
swirling in your tailwind.

Swallow the chugging
freight train of your own
insistent verifications.

The Ten of Staves

Attitudes of Others

The astronomer
on the far side of the moon
has never seen the Earth.

The aging ingénue
maintains her innocence
despite an immodest décolletage.

Your Dutch uncle
throws a surprise party
for a decadent valley.

The taxi driver
agrees to take you
to Lithuania.

The Knave of Clotted Cream, Minor Arcana

Obstacles to Overcome

The tautological torture
perambulated in
the calculation of π.

The borders of peripheral vision
as delimited by the right
hemisphere of the brain.

A towering bricolage

of torn ligaments
and distended limbs.

A Berkhausen dirigible,
circa 1937,
from the airfield at Dresden.

The Falling Sorcerer, Major Arcana 7, Reversed

Possible Outcomes

The archipelago of dream plastics
already ancient
in its pocked decay.

Outrageous success
in the arms of a statue.

Two griffins
resting couchant
before an empty throne.

Three spent shells
on the library carpet,
next to the broken flounder.

The hooves and bit
and the charred bones
of the burnt palomino.

A locomotive
arriving at the station
without its tender.

Whimsical viaducts.

Letter from the Golden Age
g. sutton breiding

The year is 2010.
It's all science fiction to me.
When I was a child, I knew, from my readings,
that by now
the starships
would be coming and going like luminous sleet.
This world—
it would be all marvels and wonders and miracles

and endless beauty.
In the mind of a ten-year-old,
these visions were true and real and permanent.

They still are.
Although the streets
are covered in shit, trash, vomit, half-dead
pigeons, cinders,
automobiles, and all forms of ugliness,
and the air I breathe is black,
although the ships never came,
my ink still burns
into the twilights
like the long, glowing contrails across
the alien skies of the future.

The waters of space still lap
at my dreams.
Time foams up.
I pluck the silver berries of the stars,
send messages in dark wax
to the monks of far Centauri,
and drink the strong wine of lipstick
from the helmets of the Astronauta.

I pluck the silver berries
and eat them quickly
like a fatal drug.
Time foams up
from the dead streets to cover
my windows as I lose myself
in theories
on the nature of sentience and image travel.

I have already been so far away,
so many times,
to the deepest reaches of space.
Yet
I still await
the violence of titanium
and the engulfing fires
of retrojets and
afterburn.

I can't say why.
But the ships,
I know,
will come.

Terraforming Mars
Benjamin Cartwright

I.
Orbits and surveys
mark the stubble and contours
of a red face—
those stubborn landscapes
of dust and canal
returned and embedded
with lenses and in pixels
until they inhabit dreams.

II.
Rovers and the fragile domes
of modules and probes.

The skitter of landers
across red plains.

The tension of caps and rocks
compressed to release

their breath, a slow exhalation.

III.
When the first rains splatter
on the skins of the domes
there will be echoes of home
in this newly pressured place—

our gift and penchant
for making a forge
out of every climate
that slips into our orbit.

IV.
The Boreal and the temperate
will take time
as the changelings in the domes
and descendants in the landers
spend centuries casting
the slender kernels
of redwood seeds
across the red face
and changing countenance
of freshly named continents.

V.
The red breath thins
and dismantles
module after module
when the frost returns

and liquid freezes
and expands with the heart,
with the sharp edge
of what is lost
like atmosphere.

The lenses and the landers
remain.

The red echo of a home
fades before the blue
and green of the first note
it mimics—

an impossible lapse
in descendants
and diminishing scales,
like a dream
where the father
outlives sons who left
for jagged coasts and unknown shores.

The 25-Cent Rocket: One-Quarter of the Way to the Stars
G. O. Clark and Kendall Evans

He was all of six years old
In 1952
When he rode a 25-cent
Rocket to the stars.

His mother
Dropped the quarter in,
The rocket's 'lectric engine
Throbbed—
Soon he was looking down
Upon the rooftops,
The supermarket's
Parking lot,

His mother gazing upward,
Shielding her eyes

Against bright sunlight,
Waving him goodbye,

"I forgot to pack your lunch,"
She called,
Her voice sounding small
& distant.

He wasn't worried, though.
There were three jawbreakers
In the deep pockets
Of his jeans.

He grips
The rocket's steering wheel
& aims for where
Red Mars might be,
Beyond the fierce blue sky,

His final destination,
Further than a budding
Imagination's reach,
Past picture-book planets
And moons
And mysteries still unnamed,

Pausing along the way
To play dodgem cars
In the asteroid belt,
Skim above
Old Saturn's rings,
And grab a sweet snow cone
On Pluto.

Out beyond the outer planets,
The swirling dark gasses,
He grips the wheel more tightly,
Steering for the stars.

But distance is deceptive,
The stars a long long way away,
Mere pinpricks of light
Seeming too small
To grow into bright suns—
Is he approaching too slowly?

It seems to take forever.
He feels bored,

Then frightened.
Is there enough fuel
To make it home again?

Like a sudden dream
His harried return trip
Swerving past Saturn,
Curving around Jupiter
Diving ever sunward
Toward Earth and

A gentle crash landing
By the supermarket
Parking lot,
Electric engines
Throbbing their last,
His mother patiently waiting
To welcome him home.

Afterwards he knows
The mountains of the moon
& the canyons on Mars
Loom close; closer
Than grownups dare believe,

But he knows the truth,
All of six years old,
Already one with the future,
One quarter at a time,
On a never-ending ride.

Postcards from Mars
C. S. E. Cooney

[**Postcard 1:** *I am here. I am safe. I am starting a garden.*]

She saved her whole life for this.
Penny-pinched from couch cracks,
Gutter garbage, bottom of the purse.
I gave my change to beggars;
She kept hers for Mars.

Clear mason jars, blue glass vases, brown
Microbrew beer bottles, heavy with her haul,
She wanted to take them all
To Virgin Galactic Gateway—
Proof of her intentions.

"Mom," I said, "let's go to the bank. Get a money order."
"Right! I'm so excited my head is spinning!"
She couldn't stop grinning.

[**Postcard 2:** *You ever see the sunset from Outer Space? I have.*]

She threw herself a funeral—
"Like Tom Sawyer only better!"
We wore:
Lily wreaths, roses on our wrists, unseemly boutonnières.
We sang:
Amazing Grace, How Can I Keep from Singing, The Blue Green Hills of Earth
Her voice soared above us like a mother ship.

I did not cry.
My eyes were dry.

[**Postcard 3:** *I go out for walks when I can. Try peeing in a space suit sometime. *gigglefit**]

Citizens of Mars are allowed one postcard a month
Part of the package, the plan,
One-way ticket to a pilgrim planet
All she could afford.

Citizens of Earth have no stamps for Mars.
I never wrote her back.
Mostly I pretended she was dead.
Like she said.

[**"We regret to inform . . . "**]

They tell me she went striding
In the uplands of Tharsis
Alone, in her borrowed gadgetry.
There was a storm.
(I did not know Mars had storms.)
And somewhere in the red, red dust—
She disappeared.

Later, they found her suit.
Like a cocoon, outgrown.
Like an empty tomb.

I escape the sound bites, read no headlines,
Stop answering my phone.
In the anchorhold of my solitude
I study her postcards—

Search for clues, secrets, whisperings
Footprints in the red, red dust.

I finish the jam, wash out the jar.
Three pennies, a dime and a quarter so far.

The Chant of the Black Cats
Lyn C. A. Gardner

We are Halloween: we black cats,
puddles that vanish into night,
our green eyes flashing like horizon light
that warns of ships that drowned
because no good-luck black cats
prowled the decks, fending off storms,
brushing sailors with midnight magic.
As Halloween cats, we keep watch
behind curtains, atop fences, underneath cars.
It's our night, and we lash our tails, puff wide,
fill hollows so deep we're only floating eyes.
A Halloween moon's best, harvest orange,
fat as a pumpkin, a gleam as sweet as pies.
We braid it into whisker-threads, weave mystic light
in a paw-dance across the path of those who need our luck.

We march in sleek black funeral attire,
a slinky but precise procession:
every step counts, spells widdershins,
ace in the hole and a paw to keep it there.
Inspired by us, you parade your young
like a lioness showing her cubs to the pride,
your own kittens wrapped in flamboyant pelts,
nudged to walk on their own to ring the bell,
present themselves, say the magic words,
a regal procession rich with ritual
that unifies you for a single night,
even the babes in arms brought close for approval,
while proud parents stand back, watching
the cubs play at hunting treats on their own.

It's the most dangerous night of the year.
Roads are always bad, but Halloween turns black cats
from hunters into prey. Tin cans and tail-burnings,
E. A. Poe hangings, living burials. House cats get trussed
in fancy clothes, protesting with ululating yowls,
distracted from their mission: to spot spirits that slide through cracks,
rousting them like rodents, vigilant to preserve

the warmth of the home, while the hard months begin outside—
frost, starvation, as mice hibernate and birds fly south—
No food banks for cats, and shelters overflow,
spelling more feline deaths.

Despite the need for our Halloween magic,
we've had to give up perching on fence posts
in orderly, obvious rows. Now we cluster
in skeletal trees where you can't get us—
wary of owls, our claws sunk deep in bark
to keep from being snatched and flown away
while above us, great horned owls chuckle:
We'll eat you, black cats, they hoot
while we hunker in the crooks of branches.

We peer down with the luster of ambers and greens,
the menacing sparkle of Halloween lights.
Velvet brushes your cheek—cold rush as our tails anoint you
with Halloween magic, the chill finger of death
to keep you on your toes. You duck and scream,
run, fleet, young again as we shiver you alive
with electric fur and fine, needle-prick claws,
slipping through night to thread our nine lives through yours
like stitches, binding the rents in your spirit,
Frankenstein's monster stitched whole and new,
pumped full of lightning, galvanized by fear.

The Witch Girl
Lyn C. A. Gardner

The witch girl crouches beside her cauldron,
chain dragging from an iron collar like a dog's.
They don't trust her yet with the bones they grind
to make their soup. They caught her gnawing, snarfing down
her own leg in the woods, starvation slimming her throat
so the bones of her ankle caught in her craw,
choking they mistook for a witch-chick's first attempt to cackle.

Now she stirs broth, the base for spells:
plastic filters from a forest fire; shards of shattered star;
Sweet William three days dead, the flesh
still succulent on his bones. He'd been rotting,
dropping pieces of himself, a dirty white trail of breadcrumbs
that the vultures and hyenas loved. The witch girl followed,
collecting him in her basket, popping his leavings in her mouth
till flesh melted from bones, sweet with his charm that won every heart.
Mother, our caravan queen, always loved him best—

she mixes his *memento mori* in every spell, small bones to remind us
of him with their delicate crunch, perhaps with a strand woven in
of those fine golden locks she doles out one by one,
keeping the rest to build the girl a husband when the time comes.

Right now the girl is barely more than feral—
fruitless to comb that storm-cloud hair or trim it with bones,
though tinsel might be nice, if any shards of broken star are left.
She's got to look frightful in case the town creeps by for thrills.
But the wild gleam in her swamp-dark eyes may be enough.
She pins you with that stare, animal malice, human deceit,
the scorn of a dirty trick, the first prick of capture
before the killing jar.

When the witches roll into town, setting up wagons under the trees,
guarded by a fence of crossed broomsticks—beware.
The witch girl lures you in, skinny child needing solace,
her gaunt, dirty cheeks aiding her pleas for staples:
An eye, perhaps? You have a spare. That great big nose? Whittle off
a few ounces. Your brain? You won't miss it. Fingers make
delicious finger-food. She's so cute, ragamuffin waif—you pity her, forget
she's already a witch at heart. Fire glares orange through the moon-cut door
behind which her sisters beckon, luring unwary rest-stop seekers
to add their exotic, well-traveled flavors to the soup.
If you're lucky, the witch girl will honor you by stretching your tattoos
from two crossed poles to catch the wind, Halloween banner
under the moon, strong scent to distract the townies till she bangs her pot
with that menacing glare: You next. They scamper.

She's more than wolf-bred—more like the slough of self-deceit,
mother-hatred, self-loathing, repudiated love, the bitter strength
of a heart turned sour, a putrid and terrifying drink.
The witch girl smites you with that killing stare,
the frank malice of her scowl, the dark night where her soul lurks.
Her tangled hair and dirt-smeared face, her bloody rags
where limbs poke through like bones, might incite sympathy
if she didn't hate you all so fiercely. It's intriguing, the way she stirs
that pot of dashed hopes with her ladle of bone. Is that your leg?

After all, you haven't come home. You cursed me last night,
before you stormed out without your keys: you'd go to the caravan
to seek your fortune—find yourself. You wouldn't wait for an umbrella,
just ran out into the sleet, yelling that it wasn't me, and what was there
to leave behind? Your defiant look so much like hers—those black eyes
full of hate. That heart-bloody sleeve. That patch of bright, gnawed bone
where you chewed yourself free of this trap, to hobble into the killing wood,
leaving me here, like the witch girl, to simmer and stew
the poison that teaches me to be glad you're gone.

Summary: Kinetic vs. Potential
Albert Goldbarth

In 1796 Elias Henshaw, who had never smoked
a cigar or a pipe or ever taken a dram of spirits
or even entered a spirited altercation, burst
spontaneously into flame—no heat source
anywhere nearby—and such was the ravenous
ferocity of the fire that, despite his friends' alacrity
with a ladled-out barrel of rainwater, he
was soon reduced to a stack of greasy ashes,
disturbing to view and rancid to whiff.
In 1854, Rebecca Norris the same. Wen Fu
and Israel Lodz the same. A famous scene in Dickens
describes the phenomenon. In 2003 an infant
five months old named Shylene Washington, in a room
devoid of the tiniest spark, a room that was,
if anything, dry and chill according to witnesses,
turned—*snap!*—into a burning, melting
shapelessness that would fit on a christening pillow,
and pool, and cool to a rubbery mass with only
a few charred bones to hint that once this thing
possessed an identity. The annals of human mystery
bear hundreds of such instances—not that

    any friend of mine has succumbed, or I'll wager
    any of yours, or any friend of those friends'; or even any
    stranger I've seen, not at the salon, or the governance meeting,
    the strip club, the news room, the sacristy,
    or at marriage counseling—no more than my own
    so-very-willing-to-be-credulous (though not
    irrational) eyes have witnessed even one of the thousands
    of reported saucers skimming like Scottish curling stones
    over sheet ice, buzzing low like electric clippers
    over the wheat, or sometimes landing on a highway in an air
    their subacoustic hum makes green (or purple) (or streaked
    throughout with snakes of light), and green (or gray) (or gray-green)
    beings emerge, "the credible witnesses include an Air Force pilot
    and a sheriff," "a van of tourists," "everybody on the plane,"
    although not me, nor have I seen the ghosts or the yeti
    or one sprung werewolf hair from a cheek, and yet
    the testimony to such things is a clamor so unending that
    the seeds of these extremities *must* be deep in us, in all of us,
    and anyway "the absence of proof," as Carl Sagan has pointed out,
    "is not the proof of absence"—an exemplification of which
    might be (remember the marriage counseling?) my friends

Shalimar and Abel, who will sit in front of their mediator
an hour at a time like milk glass figurines, so
pale and still, although you know their subatomic bonds,
if broken, would—like anyone's—release the same hellfire
that devastated Hiroshima and Nagasaki, yes, they host
their weekly dinner parties with unruffleable calm, and yet
you know their molecular makeup, the electrochemical
selves inside their selves, can't differ much from that
of the neighbor who kneels unashamed in the street to conduct
her conversations with angels, arguing, crooning, spitting, giving
off the glimmer of a torch. A woman
I knew once pointed coyly to her clit (yes, there's a background
story that really isn't a part of this) and told me something
I've always imagined being uttered by Doctor Tulp
in Rembrandt's famous "anatomy lecture" painting, as he draws
his viewers' attention down the length of a laid-out body
that's skinned to its raw, pink, fatty abundance. "Just
because it isn't burning
doesn't mean it's not a candle."

Wallpaper
April Grant

1.
Dripping with sweat, an ache in her head,
A girl wakes in a green bed,
Safe in her mother's house again,
A cloudless sky outside.

Mowers outside roared through her dream,
The blue jays flutter and scream:
A hot and baking day of May,
An hour after dawn.

Her walls are papered with crimson fruit,
Dark, tangling down their root,
Clinging to night in gray and blue.
She loved it as a child.

The room was hers before she was grown.
It's hers again, alone.
Though her dream calls, "I want, I want,"
It fades in streams of sun.

Still, staring at the wall, she lies,
Tracing patterns with her eyes—
Limbs, elbows, throats, curled roots, black hair,

Aslant, across, and down.

Mother downstairs: beginning to bake.
The scent makes her belly ache.
She has known these walls too long.
They tell her nothing now.

2.
She walks between the garden beds,
By orange-blazing marigolds.
Her mother paces at her side,
In yellow, with a broad-brimmed hat,
Smelling of scones and raisin toast,
Tall in the unabating sun.

—This is the time to buy tomato starts.
The kitchen garden faces to the south.
I'll plant it all again now that you're home.

—That sounds good, Mother.

—My peonies are reaching for the skies,
Covered in buds. We'll have a record year.
They're glad to see you. Never leave again.

—I won't, Mother.

—Didn't you eat when you were with that man?
You look as though he starved you for six months.
I'll be so glad to haul him into court.

Yes, fruit, blood, flesh,
Silence and night, I knew their taste,
Knew strength when his brutality
Bowed, gentle, at my feet.

—I'm sorry, honey, I'll stop, please don't cry.
I know, you had no choice. He broke your mind,
He forced you, with those eyes. It's over now.

—Yes.

—I'll need your help to cut the daffodils
And carry dead leaves to the compost heap.
The tulips and the hyacinths are past.

—I'm sorry.

—You're getting sunburned. Look at your poor arms.
Why can't you ask the servants for a hat?
You know they'd all do anything for you.

—I'm sorry, Mother.

—Go inside and rest.

3.
That night she walks her room,
Naked and burnt, alone at last.
The mirror by the stained-glass hanging lamp
Reflects her, merciless and clear,
The bony knees, the pale and graceless limbs,
The red and blistered arms,
The seared red skin on lids and nose.
It aches; she feels her heartbeat in her face.

Salve for her skin smells sweet:
Pine needles, smoke, and scented lands
Where they would hardly recognize her now.
She had pale servants in that place.
She was a queen and judge, before the end.
And do they think of her,
Curse her, cold woman, traitor, bitch?
Or do they all forget, as he'll forget?

The paper on the walls
Grows lush by night-time and recalls
Dark eyes between the leaves, muscles and veins,
A mouth with pomegranate stains.
She rubs against the wall, deliberate, calm,
Leaving a smear of balm.
Blue dye rubs off along her chin.
She whispers, "Lover, lover, let me in!"

Wendy Darling Has Bad Dreams
Sally Rosen Kindred

1.
Long-armed now, hard-boned
and wingless, I'm
a woman grown. Now,
not never, I live
aboveground. I don't have any children.
There's a man in this bed I might love
if he could believe

where I've been,
in the hot island of my skin
torn by wet and dirty arrows—
if he could know why I'm done
with the twill of being a girl,
with my hands drifting down
to dust the fine sleeves of boys
who want flight
from me and the fierce light
my stories gave them, want back
their first black wings.

2.
Rope bites into my wrists and I'm
in the ship again, pressed
to the sweat of blurry pirates, the heat
of their fictional whispers
draining down my hair.
For what I've wanted,
Tink wants me dead: her thin
light glares into my soft ribs.
Her glass wings hum for my blood.

My brothers twist on the bench
opposite, gagged and retching.
Peter's missing. Our mother is another country,
and we've burned the map.
The boys lift their bound
arms to me. They are mine.

3.
Peter once said I made that world. I lie
with it: guilt simmers my dreams, its ocean
seeps out in pain along my arms
when I wake forgetting
I'm home, forgetting why rain
is coming down outside
but my body's by a man's, and bone dry.

Sometimes I look across the sheet
at his sweet flesh and can't stay.
Some days my skin hurts
against anything in this world.

4.
I think now I was meant to be the clock
in the crocodile, to claim warm minutes
in the story's gut,
in the boneless dark

alone, and later,
with Hook beside me—
a kind of matrimony. We'd
lie together. In that center
I'd stop pretending the world
wasn't a mess of salt and hunger
winding down. Our words
would taste metallic, breaking
in the acids of desire. We'd be like
my heart, dirty and wild, counting
inside a body turning away from story,
dipping under the sea.

In the Third Cycle
Rose Lemberg

> *In the first cycle find a companion,*
> *in the second cycle seek dominion,*
> *in the third cycle learn humility,*
> *in the fourth cycle become yourself.*
> (a mnemonic to recompose the *Wanderings of Daie*)

The Wind Hoarder speaks of his yearning for Keddar

That young man with skin honeyed gold, that boy
with hair like heavy flax ropes, eyes like almonds,
fingers like caged nightingales, mind like a thrown knife—that young man
who poured sherbet for me when I was thirsty,
who saw me when I came, wind-wrapped, carried through the air
by my power, the power that obscures
and reins the whole world in storm's harness—that youth
who whispered to me gently, who knelt
to ask after my comfort, that boy

he belongs to my sister—

twirling shadow, long-limbed, dancing death-dance, Journeymaker,
adviser to dust kings, diviner of roads stretched under the ground, pointing
to where power aligns with the earth, sprouting
cities above ground.
        Sister mine,
you had never been greedy,
never sought consolation from strangers, or an army; alone
you traveled, following the desperate prayers
choked in mid-word: the weeping of men,
mothers' stunned silence—
sister mine,

I should not begrudge you
the young man who brought me sherbet on a hot day, who knelt
to ask after my comfort.

Keddar reminds the Journeymaker of the First Cycle

You say we've always been together
since you first walked among us, at the dawn of time;
you taught us to spin wool, and to fight
with two swords; how to forge iron
and raven feathers into nightsteel. You pulled
fire from the burning sun, tricking the gods,
and gave that fire to us. You stitched
a land that is good to wander, and taught us
to braid hair. In return,
you asked for nothing. We asked
to appease you. You asked
for me.

I lived first then,
a boy among others, a youth
with skin nut-brown from wandering
the unrelenting steppe, a youth who had smiled
readily, in that first cycle. I do not remember much—
how the grass whispered, caressing your calves when you walked
wise as the dawn and as quiet, away
from the camp, away
from my people
with me.

The Journeymaker tells Keddar about his betrayal

I wear obsidian leathers
and a belt made of spun sun.
I sang for myself
a sword, blue as the whistling thrush.
I stitch for myself
journeys
to where I am most needed.
From war to war I walk, my blade hissing skin
off my enemies, for those who pray to me
trapped desperate in silence, when the heartblood leaks
grief begotten by mothers, and is soaked
into the fabric of the earth. There, at the dawn of time,
I stitched these lands together.
No, I can't wash the war off. I only can
quilt over bewildered grief. When I journey, the land
whispers of violations,

new wars over old unhealed hurt.
Nobody hears but me.
Nobody hears. You think it's too much
to ask for your obedience? Come then, I will show you
where in the Second Cycle
your greed disgorged crows,
when, born the second time,
you turned the bloodswords I had sung for you
out of my blundering heart
against these enameled cities
their walls anointed in myrrh—the three
cities where I found respite. Now look,
these are not ruins, desolation
restful under my brother's breath—no, they stand—
the once-radiant cities crawl with vermin,
their enamel peeled, children bathe in filth,
artisans are uncaring in their craft, poets
scream raw under the burden of crippled enormous words.
Two hundred years, Keddar, two hundred years,
How am I ever to quilt this right?
You do not remember, you say? How you tore from my path
joyfully—you do not remember. Only how the blood
sang in your mouth
how the blood
sang—
Why, how convenient.

Keddar to the Journeymaker: first song of the Third Cycle

If I hold very still
folded in the bedclothes of the night,
I can hear the world breathing. Trees inhale
darkness through serrated bark. In my father's house
stones groan against the freezing air. Maids snore, and noblewomen
warm under goat-wool, snore. The whole kingdom
closed in by the Wind Hoarder's prison guard, draws
breath after pacified breath—except yours,
yours,
yours is missing.
You had lived here
stalwart by my side, guiding my steps as I grew.
I thought you couldn't speak, but now I wonder
if you refused to speak to me. We called you Raven Woman.
Harsh and shining, you would caw no fate
at my birth. You frowned
at my mistakes; but when I looked
quiet through slitted eyes, feigning sleep, I saw you
look down at me, and a smile

folded your face into softness.
Please, I can no longer sleep
under my father's roof. The herons
ruffle their chests against each other; outside, the primrose
confides in the juniper. Stone with stone,
page by illuminated page, and sword against sword,
lover to lover, the world clings together. Only your
breath is missing.

The Wind Hoarder to Keddar, of when they first met

In your kingdom, women embroider
blue eyes upon red ribbons
a ward against my thievery. They came,
giggling behind plump fingers, to watch you dance
the two-sword with your Raven Woman
and you intent only upon her; sweet beads of sweat
on your arms reflected her. When, arrayed
in screeching feathers, she left you, you lay sick
day after spurious day in the stone fortress. Hurt
seeped through your pores with the sweat.
You took to the knife one morning, slashed
dozens of ribbons from the women's garments,
summoning me to harm you. And I, a fool,
laughed, for you didn't seem to know
your name, or how you betrayed her,
or that she was my sister. I lifted you
by your hair, thick and braided into ropes; brought you
home with me to the wandering steppe of the air
to my wind-yurt, to my fur-bed of flurries.
I should have made you stay
forever in the bondage of my arms
above the cloudburst. Instead, I gave you
words to know yourself: your three rebirths,
your name, and hers. I gifted you a wind
to guide you skydown to her. When your lips pressed
warm upon my palm, I should have known. Alone
of all men and women under Skyroad, you called me
kind, you thanked me
with bashful words. A fool,
why did I let you leave? I should have known
how dear you are to me.

The Journeymaker to Keddar

There was a wood once,
a copse blue with pines,
berry-rich under the benign dawn. A small people

passed through the forest every summer. They took respite
from the scorched steppe
and drained the sweetness of the birch,
and wrote their hearts on bark. When I came among them
raven-clad,
belted in the sun's brightness,
they sang.
No, not in desperation—they sang to me
simply because I existed.
I riddled to them secrets—how to spike milk,
how to stitch hides, and to make shelter
against the onslaught of my brother's regard—but still they slept
braided to each other
beneath the benevolence of the sky.
They changed. The world changes. Why did you have to change?
What joy is there in conquest? Your people did not need it
back in the dawn of time, when the leaping trout spelled
the syllabary of the stream, when the steppe
feathered in pink blossom. Remember to me
how you made your life into that song
just because I exist—
Keddar,
and I will no longer
go without. Who else but you, how else
to darn these deeds of yours, quilt a new journey
out of our ravaged truths? My heart
a patchwork.
I should have kept it safe
inside the strongbox of my loneliness; I let it change
just like the world, when you
returned to me.

The Changeling's Lament
Shira Lipkin

I have studied so hard
to pass as one of you.
I've spent a lifetime on it.

I have tells.
Blisters, tremors, bruises,
all the signs that I was not meant for your world,
was not meant to be contained
in your clothes,
your shoes.
I have this terribly inconvenient allergy
to cold iron.

Hives, really.
Welts.
I stand out.

When I was little,
I asked my alleged mother,
what's a girl?

She said,
you,
you're a girl,
and she laced me into dresses
(that I tore off in the school parking lot,
in line for the bus).
Laced me into ballet shoes
that left blisters
and bloodied my feet
until I had calluses.
Which she had filed off,
beauticians pinning me down,
because it's not beauty
if you don't bleed.

My dancing was different.
My dancing was swaying treelike,
or launching myself across the room,
spinning madly,
but that is not what girls do,
not human girls,
not ladylike,
not contained.

And everything
is about *containment*,
is about being delicate
and pretty
laced into corsets
whalebone stays digging into your ribs
because it's not beauty
if it doesn't hurt.

But I studied.
I pretended.
I hid the bruises
and the tics.
I hid the big dark parts of me.
I tamed my hair.
I watched my mouth.

I hid my magic.
I did not speak of such things,
because we do not speak of such things—
not anger,
not homesickness,
not longing.
Not this sense
that I don't know what the hell
a human girl is
and I can tell, I can,
that everyone knows I don't belong here.
I laugh too loud;
I am too fast or slow to laugh.
I am an anthropologist in the field of girl.
I study,
but none of it
ever comes
naturally.

None of it is in my nature.

I am something larger,
more fluid,
less contained,
less constrained.
But I am stranded in this place.
I have had to learn how to live here.
I have tried.
So hard.

The Last Dragon Slayer
Elissa Malcohn

I.
She is the wet dream of every budding knight, the centerpiece of every quest. Her scaly head on a pike makes the ultimate maiden magnet. You want her scorching your shield. You want her claw for a talisman, her teeth for their magic, her treasure for your throne. Legends told and retold, manuscripts illuminated or leaded in stained glass, your likeness on coin, your imprint on progeny and land.

This is the bedtime story that keeps boys awake, for you alone must breach her lair. The king's armies stay behind. The ladies in waiting wait. You have seen the riderless horses return, stumbling as if blind, rearing at their handlers, snorting chilled foam, and known that men have turned to char. Known that a dragon slayer is what you are, savior or sacrifice, hero or trampled bones. The sweat of your mount, trotting through pageantry, carries your fear as you climb to her domain.

II.
She dreams of open spaces,
the roar of leathery wings.

Flames arcing across clouds
as the herd bellows.

Great migrations over the mountains,
hatchlings clinging to her spinal ridge.

Courtships, long necks entwined,
sizzling whispers and lifted tails.

The tiny world below,
before the apes dropped from trees

and dressed in skins, then cloth, then mail.
Before the lance, the arrow, the sword.

III.
You expected the goblets,
rubies studding hammered gold,
tossed helter-skelter over
muscle-embossed breastplates . . .

the open treasure chests
blinding with dazzle.
The arsenal of tempered blades
in would-be heroes' scabbards.

A cave ablaze in metallic light,
choked with riches floor to vaulted arch:
your fabled dragon's décor.
No one mentioned

the scraps of trouser and tunic
kept safe from blistering breaths,
or the warped planks of useless wood,
or the frayed tapestries, the errant wheels,

and all the broken bolts,
and all the crumpled kingly proclamations,
the heavy musk of old vellum
drifting in a snow of tattered flakes

as closely guarded as the wealth.

Massive piles tumbling beneath the leaps
of five dozen unincinerated cats
chasing their meals out of raised helmet visors.

IV.
Tribute
once came to her,
petitioning her strength,
her likeness waving from banners.
Rulers

bowed low
with offerings,
invoking her magic
for protection, for fattened crops.
Her breath

broiling,
cleansing to ash,
she soared above the steeds.
Manes like fire, their nostrils flared
like hers.

Kings changed.
Power dissolved.
Steel washed her kind away,
red rivers tracking tears down the
mountains.

V.
She does not smell the stink of soured wine,
mouse droppings in the joints of rusted greaves.
The rotted fruit is trivial, benign.
She holes up in her cave and never leaves.

There's barely room to move for all the trash.
There's barely time to think for all the grief.
Her gem-encrusted, fusty, broken stash
grows evermore, yet offers no relief,

nor fills the icy void within her soul.
And though men come and go, and give her chase,
their little deaths fulfill no noble goal.
Their last sight, the last member of her race.

She takes no comfort in their blackened bones.
Rough walls reflect the heartbreak in her moans.

VI.
silver gauntlet—
your reflection wavers—
a quickened pulse

VII.
You have a job to do.
Dampness makes you itch under your armor.
She barely notices.

Remains of the fallen
skitter beneath your boot,
but they are not you, although

you taste the stench they tasted,
ache as they ached to raise their might,
your fingers twitching by the hilt.

Her glassy eyes, the stiff frill at her neck
dare you to act. "Lunge," they say.
"Grab a chalice. Show your shield."

But the killing means nothing.
Not to her. Not to you.
Gold or rust, emeralds or rags, makes no difference.

Within her clutch of broken eggs,
kittens huddle,
mewling on straw.

VIII.
Your horse knows where to go, nibbling apples from the palms of mountain men. You recognize their battle scars, the calling cards of well-matched foes, story fodder over a mug of mead. Back home, the ladies in waiting continue to wait. Power continues to change hands. Coins change faces. Boys still dream.

Her lair is a shadow engulfing the camp, and now you know she hoards you, too. Living and dead, worthy and worthless, all with equal standing, none enough to matter. The young bucks fall and smoke rises from their hides. This corner of the world is yours. Those tents, these campfires, work songs broken by rolling logs. You share the quest of vanished dragon slayers guarding their cache of secrets. Beneath the stars your dreams grow whiskers, twitching toward a merciful dawn.

Beautiful Monster
Helen Marshall

1. born bigger than sin,
one big toe pushed from the womb
to test the feel of sunlight,
big feet upon the calescent earth
made new and red like a hot plate
for him, drunk-kneed, to walk.

2. if we were wise we would eat
our children, raw and fleshy,
that they may not grow so big.
we would be sharks, thick-bloated
in the loveless ocean.

3. the things he loved most:
ice cream, gum wrappers,
the nosing snuffle of wild pigs,
a world strange at sunset,
earthworms, eggshells, her.

4. tonsured bodies confuse him
with their lack of bristling,
their walking like pieces coming
together in the wrong places,
mechanically wrong, but lovely:
these curious half-children.

5. her knees were scraped on the inside,
hot-plate red and backward,
so he loved her crouching most,
her crookedness, her pure broken self.
"we are such beautiful monsters."

6. if he were wise he would have
eaten her ice-cream shoulders,
licked clean her ribcage,
but we are all fools in love.

7. she sees him slantwise
and incomplete, too big to take in
with his hair and rabbit-blood smell.
good girls do not love monsters.
his hands could break her;
joyfully, she could become pieces.

8. made eggshell-shy by love,
afraid she will startle like
a mother pig, all this rooting
in the ground with him—the noises

9. shudder them out from reverie,
her knee-straight brothers.
world stuck like a gum-wrapper
around them: he is naked, carcass-big,
stripped of the cloth of himself,

10. his presence made mechanically
wrong so that the click is crooked
as the bullet cracks his brainpan:
now the world made so strange
his earthworm brain drunk
in a loveless ocean.

a truth: he loved joyfully,
heart scraped on the inside,
beautiful monster.

Skeleton Leaves: A Collection
Helen Marshall

1. *I am thinking of aurochs and angels,*
the coarse pelt of a satyr and silken
feathers pulled taut in flight.

I look upon you—goat god, boy god—
and dream *the secret of durable pigments*,
dead leaves to inscribe with fingerling poems.

This—a patchwork palimpsest inscribed
with *prophetic sonnets* and sweet prayers,
traces of desire.

Under your skin—upon it—lies *the refuge of art*,
where my hand lingers for a moment,
two broken surfaces touching.

And this is the only immortality you and I may share,
my Peter, *my* Pan.

*

2. His soul is an atom
that dances the world into being.

*

Two is the beginning of the end.

3. élan lifting her from the covers,
drowsy, as a tiny hand tap taps the window
that was so solid now made wet
as a fish with clouded breath
from his unkissed mouth.

Who are you boy, she pauses,
and him languid by the window.
a foot touches the bed, and she
blushes at the seashell toes.
Shhhh, she whispers, you will wake them,
but he is quiet as a shadow
there in the room that was
sacred, her mother said, untouched
and untouchable, but there he is

and she knows he is a kind of shadow
pulled from her limbs like fleece,
first not there, and then wholly emerged,
heart beating, from her empty belly.
they fit so perfectly together
that something shifts and cracks inside her
like a breaking bell.

that single note,
echoed through her windpipes
and the space between lips
for him is everything.

*

*"Wendy, Wendy, when you are
sleeping in your silly bed you
might be flying about with me
saying funny things to the stars."*

4. It is easy to be eight years old
when I look on the smooth foothills of his face.
His voice bristles like an unshaved chin:
tickling syllables,
whispers of gold hair

as long as harp strings.

Peter's nose is a hooded falcon,
wings beating in a snort of laughter.

It is easy to be eight years old,
clothed in green under a hill
where the sky spirals and spirals.
Easy to forget.

"Come away, o human child. . . ."

*

5. *Wendy remembers . . .*

the chthonian-chalk-taste of London smoke
and the frightful image of Michael's slipper,
unheeded, tumbling from his curled foot.
    Peter never looked back, never glimpsed, never gleaned,
       how my heart knocked like a fly against a screen,
          bumbling, tripping, graceless.
             Why couldn't you care more,
                imp-child,
                   lambkin?

    There is a phenomenon, they say, that when an ocean liner sinks
    the weight of it sucks the swimming passengers behind—
    a certain kind of magnetism.
That was Peter flying
    and forgetting.
          Of course, you couldn't care, Peter,
                my joy.

For that was the magic of it,
      the heartlessness of it all.
    The trick to flying, you see,
        is simply to find a new kind of magnetism
        breaking the blood-tight bonds of kinship
        to float, flotsam-like, in the wake of a new vessel . . .

*

6. *the scattershot thoughts of twisting tasting body
crow, she whispers, crow.*

the tiny cannon explosions of breath
bursting lungs, straining veins with red-blood oxygen

seeping, seeping, straining through arm, wrist, finger,
and the sunlight dazzles
that brief cloth-of-gold cover to cloudy countertops
as I whiz by,

> *whisper whisper*
> *crow, crow, crow, crow, crow*

> dancing upon the still lake tip-tap mirror reflection
> of my toes pooling circles where they touch
> the broken stillness
> so light a touch

as the chill tucks along my spine, kisses my nape
and brings fingers around my chin to touch my nose

> *ah, I sing, I sing*
> *and Ah she whispers in the canals of my ears*

as bones hammer, bloodshot, against tiny drums
an entire world inside my cheeks
of toy soldier marches with a boom boom strike point rattle scrape

it is all so beautiful
the noisy echoes of chest cavity and brainpan deafening
like caves and valleys shouting back
my own voice
as I crow, crow, crow
the beauty of me.

*

7. Every morning, Mrs. Darling collects the clothes
discarded about the children's room: Wendy's frock and
sashes, John's muddied uniform, Michael's socks so tiny
they curl up like kittens in the palm of her hand. Every
afternoon, Mrs. Darling looks over these objects. She
washes, irons, folds, and tends to tears. Some days, Mrs.
Darling remarks upon the laundry, a shirt suddenly too
small, a sock mended one too many times.

> She looks upon her washing, ironing, folding
> hands, feels the too-tight skin. She knows she is
> growing older. She fears the tightness of her skin
> and alternately its looseness, the wrinkled folds.
> Some evenings, as she darns Michael's worn socks,
> she pulls the fraying yarn. She unravels the heel,
> the toe. Slowly. Some evenings she imagines tugging

out the blue veins of her hand, laying them in
a neat pile while her arms, shoulders, neck slowly
undo themselves.

It is midnight and the children sleep, pieces of their
daily life tucked quietly away in drawers and closets.
Mrs. Darling peers in through the door. The grandfather
clock chimes, and Michael stirs, drowsily turns,
exhales. It is already tomorrow.

*

*The boys on the island vary, of course,
in numbers, according as they get killed and so on;
and when they seem to be growing up,
which is against the rules,
Peter thins them out.*

8. It was simpler back then, brother,
to lie among the wolves.
                                          I always wondered,
           caught beneath the thumbnail moon,
why my eyes do not burn gold in the darkness
like his.

The knowledge of childhood:
a muzzle sharp and bristling,
teeth half-gleaming beneath his lips.

       To you, he taught the hunt—
         how to tread silent in the tall grass,
         tasting where the deer had passed.
       A wolf's gift.
To me, the night songs that caused men to turn,
 half-waking with a jerk,
  and wonder at the fear in their hearts.

                 It is the same now—
               that fear of fire,
            that love of moonlight—
though we have changed in other ways.

I will not hunt with you, brother,
for I must shed my teeth
and you still wake at my song,
caught between fear and hunger.

Brother, let me go.

*

9. staring at their slowly
metastasizing shoulders,
sometimes he wonders
if it would be charitable
to snuff out quickly
their birthday-candle lives
or let them gutter on
in caskets of flesh.

*

> *"And if he forgets them so quickly,"*
> *Wendy argued, "how can we expect that*
> *he will go on remembering us?"*

10. Always, there was this touch of fear to him,
lurking behind the acorn eyes
that flicked like a cat's tongue as he slept.

They say he was born in the curl of a tongue,
soft explosion of breath
that never formed a sentence before
     he vanished in the vowels.
Oh, she cried, oh.

They are asymptotic, never quite touching each other
though they reach towards infinity.
     He is his own circle.
She knows.
Oh, he cries, oh.

One day, she will rest her hand on his head,
whispering words in the darkness
to comfort him.
     She would teach him his name,
        if he would let her.
Oh, he would cry, oh.

*

11. Only once did he touch me,
that night we played November
with tattered blanket smelling of lavender and Ovaltine,
his thumb against a cold-taut nipple,
"Mmm, Wendy, you have such goose bumps," and I shiver,
and the blanket moves like hair across us,

thick with mother-scents I cannot recall,
neither of us knowing what parents do,
only the odd feeling of the calluses
chasing teacup breasts for warmth

> *"We've built the little walls and roof*
> *And made a lovely door,*
> *So tell us, mother Wendy,*
> *What are you wanting more?"*

lost boys snort and snore and his hand still there,
though by now his mind has wandered, so I touch
the flotsam curl of hair on his temple;
autumn breathes in through drainpipes, windows, chutes,
a single moan in the throats of our little house;
he and I curl together like flexing fingers

*

12. With the children gone, the house no longer
breathes. There are no tantrums, no sword fights and
pretending, no dinnertime lectures, no stories. Mrs.
Darling sits at the table, hands folded like a laundered
shirt, and waits. When Mr. Darling enters, she does not
look up. She disdains the steps of daily living.

> Today, Mr. Darling has stitched on his paling wife
> with a sewing needle. Now she follows him to work,
> drinks coffee as he does, reads the newspaper. As
> one, they rise from the table. As one, they mount
> the stairs, past the empty room on the left.

She knows something is wrong, but Mrs. Darling can
no longer remember the weight of her own body. It is
easier for her to live in this darkness.

*

> *She was the cannibal of the seas,*
> *and scarce needed that watchful eye,*
> *for she floated immune in the horror of her name.*

13. There is something in the darkness,
a gleaming spine,
great arcing bones, oars, ribs, veins.
The waves circled around this thing always.

> The tide drew back like linen covers,

       and this gleaming giant,
       cradled, waits.

The moon is one for secrets.
She tugs across skin and sea and sand.
There are deep scratches where she passes,
furrows in the dark stretches
large enough to hold me when I sleep.

A dark eye watching me.

       The dead never rest
       beneath the ocean.

The moon has pulled off my skin.

We are all naked;
restless ribs
flutter in movement.

       There are no words for tomorrow
       beneath the ocean.

We break open in the long stretches of silence.
Our voices escape us,
echo through the wide spaces
between bones.

We are both skinless,
you and I,
a hollow mass of whistling air
waiting to be filled.
The dead never rest,
restless ribs
and this gleaming giant
in my skin.

       *

       O man unfathomable

14. Tick tick, whispers the floating brain
chasing half-dredged slivers that slip, soundless,
into floorboards.

       Something sits half-digested,
       stewed and spasming the brainpan,
       the skull that aches for draining

Tick tick, whispers raw nerve endings
that scrape the squeezed eye sockets
with violin friction.

> where colors accrue in the dark space
> there need not be the weight
> of hanging flesh.

Tick tick, whispers the cool curved steel,
a solid lump, a nestled toothache;
the tongue tastes metallic root-hooks.

> He cannot unhinge the parts robotic—
> the twist of grating gears
> and automatic spirals—
>
> He is too much alive
> and too much dead
> to halt his clockwork brain.

*

15. she did not know,
how could she?
what his mouth meant
when it curved like that.

*

> *. . . she was too fascinated to cry out.*
> *She was only a little girl.*

16. The moonlight peeling her skin:
apple peel ringlets,
like ripples in the water
or an onion coming apart.

There were no hands,
no hot breath on the neck
where her heart was a squirming fish,
struggling.

Through the arc of glass,
a gleam of whispering light
that leapt inside her ribs,
pooling like water.

Morning is full of hollow places,

as she stitches herself together.

                *

17. He cocks his hat just so, balanced obliquely,
chin thrust out, smooth like a boy's,
and the hand shaking, you might think
from a distance, but not shaking, full of tiny
practice twitches, one hand only.

His fingers reach an octave and a half,
but he only plays black keys for me, loving
their disorder, the stabs of sound, the unevenness
of tiny hammers cocked and falling on wire.
He never learned their pattern, though he can look
at a man and know immediately if he would draw,
anger, go thick with booze, or flinch.

I watch him kick his feet up on the table,
the mud from his boots red-brown, dust playing
games in the grooves of knives, the precise
circles of condensation; he sits like a bear
to be baited or a dog gone mad in heat.

> If he cut you open, Jas. Hook,
> he would find the skin of a wolf
> and the skin of a bear beneath that,
> clastic layers of wild animal aggression
> sedimented through time and the slow pressure-
> cooker heat. He would strip you down
> and read your age through the circles
> squeezing your heart, he would read you all,
> peeled back to your sharp bones
> and that pocket of sulfur and charcoal
> waiting for the hammer to spark.

                *

18. You must bury the body, she says,
two days too late when it is already a twitching mess
half-alive with things of the ground.

He will not look at it,
though he cleans the blade with smiling precision;
Peter will not look again.

One more thing behind him,
she thinks,
as she feels the cold weight of that

gentleman hand in hers, thoroughly washed,
and praises with a motherly affection
the half-moon nails polished like steel.

      *

> *Pan, who and what art thou?*
> *I'm youth, I'm joy.*
> *I'm a little bird that has broken out of the egg.*

19. Dead:

Ed Teynte, quartermaster;
Bill Jukes, he did not scream though they say he did;
Cecco, handsome.
One, two, three.

Gentleman Starkey leapt into the sea.
Four.

Noodler, Alf Mason, Robert Mullins.
Cookson (Black Murphy's brother),
William Slank, Morgan's Skylights.
Smee, sometimes he was kind.

Him.

I shall not count further.

      *

> *"I forget them after I kill them,"*
> *he replied carelessly.*

20. There is an Auschwitz,
she thought,
in that little boy.

      *

21. Once upon a time there was no Mrs. Darling.
There was a space where she used to be that sat cold
and empty like a furnace gone out. Mr. Darling could
hardly remember, forgot her more and more each day.
His heart was a cabinet of curiosities, so many things
missing. He cradles a child's finger-bone to his chest,
a stuffed crocodile, the scale of a fish. He cannot tell
where they belong now, only that some kind of natural
history has vanished and without it the world is chaotic,

brutal.

>   Once upon a time there was no Mrs. Darling, and
>   when the children crowd through the bedroom window,
>   no one greets them. Michael begins to cry. He
>   does not know why, only that the room is strange
>   and dark. Wendy hushes him, takes his hand, draws
>   him close. It is only Peter who knows that all mothers
>   are make-believe. "Come away. Come away.
>   There is no one here."

Wendy touches the bedspread. It is neat and folded.
This means nothing to her.

>   *

22. Some nights are lonely.

>   *it had seemed such a long year of waiting to her.*

I strip off my clothes quietly,
my skin, the layers of veins and muscle and tissue;
I leave them in a neat pile
beside my bed.

On those nights,
when I am lonely,
there is a howling deep in my belly,
in the place you never touched.

I go roaming,
my wolf-self naked,

And we run, you and I,
without our skins.
With only teeth and tongues
over the wide places where we could never touch.

I can feel you at my throat.
I can feel your breath
on the soft hairs of my body.
I can taste you.

At home,
our skins lie in neat, little piles
untouched
by teeth or tongue.

>   *

23. I know they are not real—
can never be—
these visions in the water.
Still, there is a part of me
forever caught
by that picture of myself,
dark as tea leaves
or a python's skin.

>   Ceaselessly tracing the ripples,
>   the thousand selves I could have been,
>   it is so easy to lose myself
>   in the current of possibilities
>   until I no longer hear your name
>   endlessly echoing.

*

24. Spring has lost luster
beneath the egg-white gleam of her eye.
Milk-eyed, she dreams those branches
and the arching space of roots
like cradle bars
where she used to lay her head.
> *Whoever has no house—*
> It is gone now, he whispers—
> *now will never have one*
tossed high beyond the foothills
of stunted fingers.

Broken things are better,
and he hates the clean, perfect shape
of the nightgown.
Its lack of tongues alarms him.
> *Whoever is alone—*
> who will kiss your feet, Wendy, your knees?—
> *will stay alone.*
She is stitched so firmly
to the fabric of this new life.

Once you mixed blood with milk
and tasted acorns and earthworms,
all that quiet newness in your mouth:
the broken stone that cuts sharply, cleanly.
You, Wendy bird,
> *will sit, read, write*
> the strange cruelties we rejoiced in

>   *long letters through the evening.*
Why does the latch rest firmly
where my shadow used to pass?

The dream still haunts her shuffled mornings:
the hollow space of the pram,
warm pillow and sweetly damp blankets
grown flat and shapeless as an ocean.
Her fingers curved to hooks that search
>   *and wander on the boulevards,*
>   twitching their telegraph loss
>   *up and down.*
His breath balloons the window,
but she shuts tight the curtain.

>   *

25. There is no mist in the city,
no sparks that flicker beyond your gaze
like the eyes of the first woman you loved.
Electricity has replaced fireflies
as the primary source of light.

Who needs a trail of breadcrumbs
to navigate the London tube?
There are easier ways to travel
than in a house on chicken legs
at seven leagues a stride.

Your shadow has escaped you,
and without a needle and thread,
it shall roam free. It knows her,
the first woman you loved,
knows how to find her braid of hair
dangling from the tenth-story window,
knows the name to call.

One night, perhaps, you shall turn a corner
to see them dancing:
his hand upon her hip.
He is sharper in her gaze,
and though you trace his steps
(the steps you learned together),
her smile is only for him.
You are but a shadow
cast upon the street.

>   *

26. He is brightness caught for a moment,
flickering out
as the world sheds darkness
in its skin.

The Walking Man Goes Looking for the Sons of John: Six Cantos
Elizabeth R. McClellan
(For Betsy Phillips, who knows how the roads lie.)

I.
The Devil is a good old boy at heart
who wishes sometimes he knew how to live right
but just can't stay off the stuff
of this world long enough to get saved.
After the Fall it's a long way to rock bottom.

Times have changed, but the Devil keeps
his patterns—same riffs but
the age shows in the wrinkles of his tunes.

Someone in this story's always named
for that good old-time beloved apostle,
a mostly forgotten charm
to remind babies "God is gracious"
when they have so many reasons to doubt.

When the Devil hangs around
Mississippi at midnight, he still picks
out-of-the-way intersections.
When no one comes to trade,
he sings for himself.

Every time he slips into gospel
in the middle of laying down
the most outrageous slow-time blues,
he tells himself it's pure irony, but

the way the Devil sings
*Looked over Jordan and
what did I see*, anyone would guess

the old man knows his morning train
ain't *never* pulling in.

II.
When the Devil's been drinking he forgets
how he and Robert fell out. Memphis

knows his weaknesses, laid its streets
out to confuse him, keep him wandering
endlessly up and down Beale, tipping bartenders
sooty twenties for helpful advice.

When he comes, you'll know him, whoever he asks for.
These days he smokes Camel filters. Send him
to the bar furthest up the street. Take his money but
never invite him in.

It passes with the classic
urban legend pattern. Still, that's what
Janelle with the braids who works the window bar
at B. B. King's got told, two managers ago now.
He made her promise,

made her swear on her own fool soul
to lie steadfastly to a little, lost old man
looking for his dead friends—but
in this economy in a right-to-starve state
she gave a little to get her little.

When the Devil came, he didn't want cigarettes,
just asked if Robert was inside.
When she gabbled out her set piece,
he nodded, passed her a twenty,
gagged her with the stink of rotted eggs
and something worse,

that sick organic reek of Delta alleys
when the dumpsters are all cooking
in exhaust and hundred-degree heat,
teeming with the unpleasant realities that
keep what's dead from staying around forever.
It got in her hair, worse than cigarette smoke.

The garbage smell washed out after a while, but
Gracie at the beauty shop asked if she'd gone over
to Hot Springs, looked at her strange when she said no.

Now when he comes she smiles and
tells him politely where she thinks Robert's at,
pointing him anywhere management rips off
the staff, where a spare twenty bucks
might feed two for a week.
She seals his tips in a Ziploc,
runs them through the washer
with her uniform after work.

More and more often she finds herself
dropping the crisply laundered bills
in the collection plate or the cup
of the street-face who sings, plays guitar,
likes his Jack, occasionally screams
a pitch-perfect train whistle into the night.

III.
In Nashville the Devil's been spotted
asking for his friend Johnny, getting
endless shots of Walker for his trouble.

It starts with *Join your friends
while you got 'em 'cause you know
they're getting fewer every day*,
his hat filling up with crumpled cash
from those who feel compelled to pay
but don't stop to listen.

It always ends with him
sitting on the plaza calling
shall we gather at the river
to the toxic stream below.

He thinks he's seeing double but
it's just the Shelby Street Bridge,
confusing him again.

After the flood at least twelve waitresses
reported him missing, not knowing
the river-smell that lingers in the District
will keep him scarce for a while yet.

IV.
When Elvis died the Memphis streets filled up
with mourners who didn't know or care
where their sovereign stole his rock and blues.

Moths and flames have nothing on
the Devil and wakes. It's a compulsion.

A sobbing white Jane from Michigan pointed
the wrinkled black man in the dusty suit coat
up November 6th Street when he asked,
looking lost, where Tommy was playing tonight.

*I don't think that movie
is still in theaters, is it?*

In the antique shop that replaced Blues Alley
that last time it burned down, the roof beams
still show the char. The Devil forgets this is
his handiwork, doesn't recall the August night
in seventy-seven when he spewed brimstone
and moonshine all over the floor

when the dead voice rang loud in his head
twelve gates to the city all square wide,

all the bottles behind the bar catching fire
at once, the roof showering sparks
like confetti on the street-side funeral cortege
honoring their self-styled king with tears and sweat,
a thousand pinpricks of blood sacrifice to the mosquito cloud.

Sometimes now he goes there, looking,
ends up buying old switch knives and harmonicas,
battered banjos, fiddles, guitars. They tell him, *Sir,
the blues bar moved to Front Street*, but it's too close
to the river, makes the Devil itch under the creases of his hat,

so he ends up back down Beale, smoking cigarettes
in the alley, staring holes into a plastic cup of beer
that sometimes melts clean away from his heat,
leaves a steamy puddle of regret, vinegar,
and burnt plastic for the street cleaners.

V.
Around Easter he usually swears
he's gonna give it up, goes slow and aching
down the old stage road to The Rock,

Georgia, where there's only one crossroads
and not a package store anywhere in fifty miles.
He slumps on the red clay that hisses and sets hard
beneath him, leaned up against a signpost,

coughing tar, looking up guilty as homemade sin
while he picks, hums *Could my zeal no respite know,*
ears buzzing with flies, the start of a hangover.

Even the lightning won't come to listen;
the damp air sours the strings,
but the rain won't break.

VI.
The Devil's tears are so dry they sizzle hot holes
in the wide lapels of his centenarian suit. He walks
until the moon sets, down Highway 36
to the old Cedar Grove cemetery where
the coffin fragments stick out of the earth and
the paper markers left over from the forties

look like dried yellow flowers on the graves.
The Devil doesn't need to read them, he
remembers who rests here in his bones.
Those who never got a decent burial
have always been his particular kin,
whether or not they were among the saved.

He calls the sun up with his private lamentation
for Robert, for Tommy, for all the forgotten names
of all the unnamed dead beneath his feet who

got home at the end of days, never mind
hell or high water. Licks make the leaves tremble,

last fair deal gone down.

Tender Aliens
Joanne Merriam
(after Gertrude Stein)

i.
A ship is made sometimes. Search a quadrant. A planet, any light is a sign and there is no remembrance of past meetings.

Supposing future meetings. Men have guns and our planet and we have no breath. Is a device to prevent the future necessary.

A dark crescent, a yellow sun, a moon. Draw a circle, choose an angle, account for an estrangement from matter. Account for their sun. Make the vibrations freedom and no error in patience, no error in slow. Yellow, what is yellow, is it warm, is it circling, is it a place. The faster there is movement, the faster freedom is measurement, the faster the crescent is blue-green. Please be a dark crescent. Please be a yellow sun. Please be a moon with a flag. A transfer.

An ocean and a wave and a whale on a wave and the yellow sun on a wave and a boat on a wave.

A porpoise and humans and a camera and paper and a greeting.

ii.
Gravity is something weight deposits which shows in measurements we have questions. A planet has that freedom. Is this constant. Who is this man. Language is something that frustrates what will be good.

A helicopter and clouds and a white building and guns and men in navy suits.

Walking and bowing and an introduction to hats and eyeglasses and tiramisu. Is tiramisu a cloud is chocolate a language is food a greeting.

In any human dwelling a top and bottom and frequently windows. Very likely windows are a language. Windows comprise change without themselves changing, some increase in weather describes their usefulness, the hat is a barrier to the yellow sun. It is not worn indoors.

A cup is a welcome. A handshake is a welcome. A tongue and salt and more tiramisu and broccoli and potatoes are a welcome. We have food in common. Language on time and gravity is glowing. Beyond the horizons are many simultaneous moons and suns.

Supposing a device can be made to prevent the future. Should it be made. Is it necessary. If there is a device then there is a theory and if a theory then error and if error then what.

A helicopter and clouds and salvage and our ship and their ship. A ship is a ship no matter whose. A ship is a ship is a ship is a ship and they have questions. Time is something age deposits which shows in measurements. Gravity is something and so is language. The question arises from an ocean and a wave.

iii.
Music is planed wood polished to glow. A parrot talks about time and crackers. The women wear hats indoors breaking the prohibition on hats indoors. Dresses are red and yellow with whimsical stitching.

Should it be made supposing the future is the enemy of good. Supposing in the future it can't be made. The present is the only possible time for decision. Supposing in the future helicopters and guns and men in navy suits make a transfer. Men have guns and our planet and we have no loving no questions no tongues no breath.

A beach is many grains and waves and a hat is optional. Alcohol and paper umbrellas and the removal of clothing is a greeting. The men are pale. The women swim like porpoises. The sun on a wave is yellow, what is yellow, is it blinding, is it entropy, is it the lemon in my drink. These people are beautiful and if we believe it is necessary there must be an error. Why else is blue-green so agreeable, why else is the yellow sun so warm, why else are the waves so pleasurable.

At night the window is a mirror.

iv.
A helicopter and guns and clouds and a fire on the ground. A bullet and a propeller blade and a tilting and an explosion. Are windows still windows when the glass is broken. Running and falling and a broken arm and a man with fatigues and grenades and one of their children on the ground. A broken toy in a pool of blood.

Pain is a language.

Our ship in the sky. A last transmission: by coming here we caused what we fear. By coming here we made it necessary.

No dark blue-green crescent no yellow sun no moon no ocean no waves no whales no boats no porpoises no humans no music no parrots no tiramisu no lemon drinks no white buildings no cameras no papers no windows no planet no future no red and yellow dresses.

To be, to be left, to be left behind, to be left behind to be, to be left behind to be a gate, to facilitate a transfer, to be circling, to be broken, to be hurt, to regret, to betray. To smash windows and cups, to wear hats indoors. Supposing there are more of us coming. One with that necessary device.

Snowmelt
Mari Ness

1
The dark blood glittering on the gray snow—

2
and the memories, swarming like thin crows
over fresh corpses. Your throat burns. No. *Those—*

3
cold secrets stay dying within your mind,
never quite willing to remain confined.
You know better than to think of life as kind.

4
Drop, drop. Fly to the woods,
        oh wicked crow
   a delicate heart beats
          upon the snow.

5
The mirror croons an unending song.
Black feathers gather upon the gray snow.
    I know what does and does not belong.
Black feathers gather upon the gray snow.
The mirror croons an unending song.

6
And inevitable—oh yes, oh yes—
that you should seize that apple from her hand,
its taste on your tongue almost a caress.

Inevitable that her sweet command
sucked away, for a moment, all distress.
Crows sing sadder songs in this haunted land.

7
Mother, mother. A soft cry
breaking the night.
Mother, mother. No reply.
The walls gleam a cold, calm white.

You never knew her name, nor why
the walls seemed so suddenly tight,
and the water you sipped seemed dry.

8
She came to you both in the cool moonlight:
hair white as snow, lips bloodied as a rose.
Oh, those lips, promising such rich delight!
She came to you both in the cool moonlight.
He imprisoned her hands, and crooned. Sparrows
huddled on the soft earth, afraid of flight.
She came to you both in the cool moonlight,
hair white as snow, lips bloodied as a rose.

9
And you will have time to remember all
the little men, the ebony and glass,
the frightened huntsman with his golden call,
the taste of thin gold shielding cold brass.

    The blood sinks so swiftly into the snow.

And you will have to examine each,
to twist it into some innocent tale,
a mirrored truth, a grim lesson to teach,
your cold secrets wrapped in a storied veil.

10
Sing the songs your mother knew:
    of women and dragons,
    of princes and wagons,
    of the way that the cuckoo flew
    to the only nest she ever knew.
                      Sing, crow, sing.

Sing until you make it true:
    of a bubbling witches' brew
    of poison kept in crystal flagons.

                      Sing, crow. Sing.

11
You tiptoe, so gently, to the dark woods,
to the secret places tangled in roots.
So easily we cling to our falsehoods
of warmth, of safety, of a mother's bliss
in a daughter. A needle pricks your skin.
You tuck leaves into a tattered bodice,
wrap yourself warmly in bloodied deerskin.
You were never woken with a soft kiss,
tangled as you were with other pursuits.
So easily we lose our childhoods.
The spring snows, melting, pierce your slender boots.

12
And you will remember the red hot shoes
So lovingly made with iron fire.
And you will remember that delightful ruse:
None of those tales were about desire,

so lovingly made with iron fire.
(Fingers tap at your arm, touching that bruise.)
None of those tales were about desire.
You will not use that timeworn word, abuse.

Fingers tap at your arm, touching that bruise.
And you will remember the red-hot shoes.
You will not use that timeworn word, abuse.
And you will remember that delightful ruse.

13
The crystal coffin shaking in the snow,
the mirror crooning to a lonely crow,
the prince smiling at an unmoving bride,
the huntsman knowing of uneaten pride.

These are not stories you have wished to know.

You remember waiting at the window.
The falling snow, the heat rising inside.
You remember the stinging of your thumbs.
Crows peck at the bloody snow.

The silver needles flashing to and fro.
The delicate shrouds for those who had died.
You remember hearing *She comes, she comes*
Crows peck at the bloody snow.

14
The crows arrive, spiraling, one by one,
attacking the first green shoots on the trees,
calling for their kin in the cold gray sun.
You gather large handfuls of moist, dead leaves.

You bury them all, in the half frozen earth:
the comb, the ribbon, the old apple core,
the ebony panel. Nothing of worth.
The cold dying secrets that you once bore.

And the crows flying in circles above,
the air filling with the weight of their cries,
the woods filling with the weight of true love,
the glass coffin cracking before your eyes.

And it is time, past time, for you to go.
The blood sinks so swiftly in the spring snow.

Ragnarok
Paul Park

There was a man, Magnus's son,
Ragni his name. In Reykjavik
Stands his office, six stories,
Far from the harbor in the fat past.
Birds nest there, now abandoned.
The sea washes along Vesturgata,
As they called it.
                     In those days
Ragni's son, a rich man,
Also a scholar, skilled in law,
Thomas his name, took his wife
From famished Boston, far away.
Brave were her people, black-skinned,

Strong with spear, with shield courageous,
Long ago.
           Lately now
The world has stopped. It waits and turns.
Fire leaps along the hill.
Before these troubles, Thomas took her,
Black Naomi, belly big,
To Hvolsvollur where he had land,
A rich farm before the stream,
Safe and strong.
              In the starving years,
There was born, Thomas's son,
Eirik the African, as they called him.
Hard his heart, heavy his hand
Against the wretches in the ruined towns,
Bandits and skraelings beyond the wall,
Come to plunder, kill and spoil,
Over and over.
           Every night,
Thomas stands watch, wakeful and sure,
Guarding the hall with his Glock Nine.
Forty men, farmers by day,
Cod fishermen from the cold coast,
Pledge to shelter, shield from harm
What each man loves, alone, together
Through the winter.
             When spring thaws
The small boughs, buds unpack
From the red earth. Eirik passes
Into the fields. The fire weeds
Move around him, arctic blooms
And purple bells. Below the ricks,
He finds Johanna, Johan's daughter,
Guests at the farm.
             At his father's house
He'd sometimes seen her, slim and fair,
Ripening too, a tall primrose.
He draws her down with dark hands,
Meaning no harm, but honor only.
Rich is her father, in Reykjavik,
Rich is her cousin, with cod boats
In Smoke Harbor.
           Happy then,
Proud Naomi offers her hall
For the wedding feast, but she's refused
For no reason. Rather instead
Johanna chooses the little church
At Karsnes, close to home,

South of the city along the shore.
High-breasted,
                Snake-hearted,
Sick with pride, she predicts
No trouble. Near that place,
In Keflavik airport, cruel Jacobus
Gathers his men, gap-toothed Roma,
Thieves and Poles, pockmarked and starving.
The skraeling king calls for silence
In the shattered hall.
                    Shards of glass,
Upturned cars, chunks of concrete
Make his throne. There he sits
With his hand high. "Hear me," he says
In the Roma language, learned from his father
In distant London. "Long we've fought
Against these killers. Ghosts of friends
Follow us here."
                Far to the east,
Black Eirik, in the same hour,
Walks by the water in Hvolsvollur.
By the larch tree and the lambing pens,
Thomas finds him, takes his sleeve,
Brings his gift, the Glock Nine
With precious bullets, powder and brimstone
From his store.
             Father and son
Talk together, until Naomi
Comes to find them. "Fools," she calls them.
(Though she loves them.) "Late last night
I lay awake. When do you go
To meet this woman, marry her
Beyond our wall? Why must you ride
To far Karsnes?"
               Cruel Jacobus
Waits to answer, in Keflavik,
Hand upraised. "These rich men
Goad us to act. Am I the last
To mourn my brother, mourn his murder?
The reckless weakling, Thomas Ragnisson,
Shot him down, shattered his skull
Outside the wall
             In Hvolsvollur,
With his Glock Nine. Now I hear
About this wedding. His black son,
Scorning us, splits his strength,
Dares us to leave him alone in Karsnes
In the church. Christ Jesus

Punishes pride, pays them back
My brother's murder!"
                        At that moment
Black Naomi bows her head,
Tries to agree. Eirik turns toward her,
Groping to comfort. "God will protect
The holy church. Hear me, mother,
Jesus will keep us, Johanna and me."
Then he strips the semiautomatic
From its sheath.
                    Some time later
Embracing her, he unbolts, unlocks
The steel door, draws its bars,
Rides north beneath the barrier,
Built of cinderblocks and barbed wire,
Twenty feet tall. With ten men
He takes the road toward Reykjavik,
West to Karsnes
                On the cold sea.
There the pastor prepares the feast,
Lights the lamp in the long dusk.
In the chapel porch, pacing and ready,
Eirik waits, wonders and waits.
Where's the bride, the wedding party?
Where's her father, fat Johan?
No one knows.
                Night comes.
Checking his watch, counting the hours,
Eirik frets. At first light
He rides north through the ruined towns,
Empty and burned, broken and looted.
Abandoned cars block his path.
The hill rises to Hallgrimskirkja
At the city's heart.
                    Here at the summit
Above the harbor, the high tower
Jabs the sky. Johan's hall,
Rich and secure, is silent now.
The dogs slink out the door,
Baring their teeth, biting at bones.
At Leif's statue we leave our horses,
Wait for something,
                    Sounds from the hall.
The concrete porch piles to heaven.
The door's wrenched open, all is still.
No one shouts, issues a challenge
As we approach. Eirik the African
Draws his pistol. The danger's past.

No one's left. We know for certain
On the threshold.
                   There inside
Lies Thorgeir Grimsson, throat cut.
We find the others, one by one,
Among the benches in their marriage clothes.
The bleached wool, black with blood,
Polished stones, stained with it.
Windows broken, birds fly
In the tall vault.
                Eirik, distraught,
Watches the birds wind above him,
Strives to find her, fair Johanna,
Where she lies. Ladies and bridesmaids
Died in a heap, huddled together,
Peeled and butchered at the pillar's base.
She's not there; he searches farther
Up the aisle.
              Underneath
The high altar, he uncovers
Fat Johan, father-in-law,
But for this. There's his body,
Leaked and maimed below the organ,
The wooden cross. Cruel Jacobus
Tortured and killed him, kidnapped his daughter
Twelve hours previous.
                   Proud Eirik
Turns to listen in the long light.
Out in the morning, his men call
Beyond the door. Desperate to leave
The stinking hall, holding his gun,
He finds them there. Fridmund, his friend,
Shows what they caught outside in the plaza,
A wretched skraeling
                      Skulking on Njalsgata,
A teenaged boy, bald already,
Back bent, black-toothed,
Hands outstretched. Stern and heavy
Eirik stands over him, offering nothing
But the gun's mouth. Meanwhile the boy
Lowers his head, laughs at his anger,
Spits out blood.
                "I expect you know
All that happened. Here it was
That King Jacobus carried the girl,
Stole her away, struggling and screaming,
Kicking and cursing when he kissed her.
Now he's punished, proud Johan,

Who took this church, chased us away,
Made it his hall.
                    Who among us
Steals such a thing, thieves though we are,
Jesus' house, Hallgrimskirkja?
Now you threaten me, though I'm helpless,
With your Glock Nine. Go on, shoot me.
Cunt-mouth, coward—I dare you.
Jesus loves me. Laughing, I tell you.
Fuck you forever."
                    Fridmund Bjarnsson
Pulls back his head, bares his throat.
But the African offers a judgment.
"Murder's too kind. Cut him loose.
Let him crawl to his king, Jacobus the Gypsy.
If he touches her, tell him I'll kill him.
Bring him this message . . . "
                              But the skraeling
Spits on his boots. "Say it yourself,"
The boy scolds. "Better from you.
Besides, you'll see him sooner than me
If you ride home to Hvolsvollur!"
Furious now, fearing the worst,
Eirik Thomasson turns from him,
Shouts for his horse,
                    A shaggy gelding,
Stout and faithful. Sturla's his name.
Climbing up, calling the others,
Eirik sets off, out of the plaza,
Down the hill. Dark are his thoughts,
As he rides east, hurrying home
Under Hekla, the hooded mountain,
Steaming and boiling.
                    Sturla toils
Along the asphalt, eighty kilometers,
All that day. Dark is the sky
When Eirik and Sturla, outstripping the rest,
Reach the farm. The fire burns
Under the clouds. Clumps of ash
Fall around them. Furious and empty,
Eirik dismounts.
                    Without moving,
He stands a minute by Sturla's flank
And the split wall. Waiting, he listens
To the strife inside. Soon he unlimbers
The precious gun, the Glock Nine,
Checks the slide, checks the recoil,
Stacks the clip with steel bullets.

Gusts of rain
           Gather around him.
Thunder crashes. Then he begins.
A storm out of nothing strikes the gate.
Men die among the horses,
Shot in the head with hollow-points,
Shot in the mouth for maximum damage.
They shake their spears, scythes and axes,
Swords and brands.
           In the burning rooms,
Eirik kills them. By the cold stream,
The crumbling barns, he kills more.
Howling they turn in the hot cinders.
Clip empty, he cannot reload,
Seizes instead a skraeling axe.
They circle around him, certain of triumph,
Not for long.
           Near the porch
Of his father's hall, he finds their leader,
Pawel the Bull, a Polack giant.
Stripped to the waist, he stands his ground.
Sword in hand, he swears and bellows.
Tattooed and painted, he paws the mud.
Now he charges, cuts and falters,
Falls to his knees,
           Face split,
Lies full-length. Lightning strikes
On Hekla's side. Howling with rage,
The skraelings escape, scatter in darkness.
Come too late, we can't catch them,
Let them go. Gathering hoses,
We pump water, wet the timbers
In the rain.
           Or we roam
Among the dead, drag them out
From the burned hall. Here they lie
On the wet ground, wives and children,
Old men. Naomi stands
Among the living, leans away,
Turns her face. Thomas is there,
Blood spilled,
           Body broken,
With the others. Eirik lays him
By the fire. Fridmund Bjarnsson
Finds the gun, the Glock Nine
Buried in mud, by the stream.
"Here," he says, holding it up.
"I was scared the skraelings took it.

Thank Jesus—"
                    There by the fire,
Eirik rebukes him. "Bullshit," he says.
"Close your mouth." He climbs the porch,
Raises his hands. Red are the doorposts,
The frame behind him, hot with sparks.
"God," he repeats, "God be thanked.
You know Johan, for Jesus' sake,
Took for his house
                    Hallgrimskirkja,
On the hill. He thought Jesus
Could sustain him, could preserve him,
Save his daughter—don't you see?
I also, Eirik the African,
Sank my faith in something empty—
Thomas's gun, the Glock Nine,
Chrome-barreled,
                    Bone grip.
But look now. Neither Jesus
Nor my Glock is good enough.
The rich hide behind their walls
In Hvolsvollur. Who comes to help?
But I will hike to Hekla's top,
Hurl my gun, heave it down
Into the steam,
                    And the steel bullets
After it. In the afternoon
I'll wreck this wall, winch it apart.
Safety is good, grain in the fields,
Greenhouse vegetables; vengeance is better.
This I tell you: Time was,
We were happy, here in Iceland.
Cod in the sea,
                    Snow on the mountain,
Hot water in every house,
Cash in our pockets, planes and cars,
The world outside, waiting and close.
Old men remember, mumble and mutter—
That time's gone, turned forever.
The pools are drained, dams breached,
Turbines wrecked,
                    Ruined engines
Starved for oil. The sea rises
Beyond Selfoss. You have seen
Thousands die, tens of thousands—
The mind rebels, breaks or bends.
Days ahead, the dim past,
Forward, backward, both the same,

Wound together.
                  At the world's end,
Jormungand, the great worm,
Holds his tail between his jaws.
Ragnarok rages around us
Here, tonight, now, forever,
Or long ago. Good friends,
Remember it: men and skraelings
Fought together
            Ages past.
So—tomorrow we'll march west
To Keflavik. Jacobus waits.
We'll scour the coast, search for fighters,
Heroes to help us, guide us home.
Left behind, you'll learn of us,
Tell our legend, teach the truth
Or invent it
         The old way.
Parse our lines upon the page:
Two beats, then pause.
Two more. Thumping heart,
Chopping axe, and again.
Not like the skraelings, with their long lines
Of claptrap, closing rhymes—
Not for us.
       No more.
Johanna's alive. How I know,
I don't know. Don't ask.
But I swear I'll bring her here,
Avenge this." Then he's silent,
Standing near the spitting fire,
Under Hekla, in the rain.

Girl Hours
Sofia Samatar
(For Henrietta Swan Leavitt)

Notes
In the 1870s, the Harvard College Observatory began to employ young women as human computers to record and analyze data. One of them, Henrietta Swan Leavitt, discovered a way to measure stellar distances using the pulsing of variable stars.

Quotations are from George Johnson's *Miss Leavitt's Stars: The Untold Story of the Woman Who Discovered How to Measure the Universe* (W. W. Norton, 2005).

Harlow Shapley, director of the observatory, reckoned the difficulty of astronomical projects in "girl hours"—the number of hours a human computer would take to obtain the data. The most challenging projects were measured in "kilo-girl-hours."

Conclusion
You were not the only deaf woman there.
Annie Cannon, too, was hard of hearing.
On the day of your death she wrote: *Rainy day pouring at night.*

Oh bright rain, brave clouds, oh stars,
oh stars.

Two thousand four hundred fires
and uncharted, unstudied,
the hours, the hours, the hours.

Body
        The body is a computer.
        The body has two eyes. For the body, the process of triangulation is automatic. The body can see the red steeple of the church beyond the trees. Blackbirds unfold as they grow nearer, like messages.
        The body never intended to be a secret.
        The body was called a shining cloud, and then a galaxy. The body comforted mariners, spilt milk in the southern sky. The body was thought to be only 30,000 light-years away.
        The body is untrustworthy. It falls ill.

> *The thought of uncompleted work, particularly of the Standard Magnitudes, is one I have had to avoid as much as possible, as it has had a bad effect nervously.*

        The body sits at a desk. A high collar, faint stripes in the white blouse. In this rare photograph, the body is framed in light. The gaze is turned down, the hand poised to make a mark. The body says: "Take photographs, write poems. I will go on with my work."
        The body is not always the same, the body varies in brightness, its true brightness may be ascertained from the rhythm of its pulsing, the body is more remote than we imagined, it eats, it walks, it traverses with terrible slowness the distance between Wisconsin and Massachusetts, the body is stubborn, snowbound, the body has disappeared, the body has left the country, the body has traveled to Europe and will not say if it went there alone, the body is generous, dedicated, seated again, reserved, exacting, brushed and buttoned, smelling of healthy soap, and not allowed to touch the telescope.

        The body gives time away with both hands.
        The body, when working, does not know that time has passed.
        The body died in 1921.

The body's edges are so far from one another that it is hardly a body at all. We gather the stars, and we call them a body. Cygnus. The Swan.

Introduction
Twelve o'clock.
My husband and children asleep.

To chart one more star, to go on working:
this is a way of keeping faith.

Draw me a map.
Show me how to read music.
Teach me to rise without standing,
to hold the galaxy's calipers
with the earth at one gleaming tip,
to live vastly and with precision,
to travel
where distance is no longer measured in miles but in lifetimes,
in epochs, in breaths, in light-years, in girl hours.

A Masquerade in Four Voices
Alexandra Seidel

Come, Mother, braid my hair. My dress hangs ready on its frame, emeralds entwined in silk, turquoise sea wrangled free from merfolk's grasp and purples rich as plums. I have waited for this dress long, oh so long, and my hair has grown for it, is ready to be woven like sheep wool on a loom, is ready to become a tower under your hands, is willing to shine. Darken my eyes with kohl at last and drain into my lips the richness of apricots. Kiss me one last time, Mother, and mold the mask to my skin; I am ready now to go to the

Balls are made halfway at least in dreams. This, my child, is one of their many secrets. Also, beneath the silk and brocade and the shimmering masks, these are really just humans, mostly anyways. I have worn the mask of jokers in many a dream, but I should think that the King of Time is a first for you, is it not? Scarlet suits you, after all, you look quite the gentleman prize. Let nobody ever tell you that you do not

Belong to this feast, this festivity, this magic, for just one night! Who with the breath still in their lungs could not want this? The young ones are so eager, the veterans distinguished and those who only visit for the night, well, they are quite

Choosing one of them to dance with you, to hold them close and let their lace lick my footsteps' echo on the dance floor, there is nothing quite as sweet as this. Of course the lace and silk are only half the price paid for dancing here, the shoes of silver glass only part of the subtlety required. Whatever happens while the moon is in the sky, nobody ever parts with their

Masks everywhere, like echoes of rain in the mountains. Mother, if only you could see this! I have left home, but feel like I am home again among the candlelight and the frankincense in the air, among the masks of eagles and of sorcerers, unicorns and lions, birds with plumage red as

Blood is so sought after. You must understand this. It is a ball, a masquerade after all, and thus as much a hunt as all of these things put together. All of them want to draw first blood, thinking that it will make them brave and exalted, but they fail to realize that this first bead of ruby may be their own. So, you see, while scarlet suits you, it also condemns you, King of Time, to the longing in their

Eyes are ever on you here. They must be, or else this would not be a ball that could hold those of my standing amongst the heavens, not even for the space of a cup of wine. Mine is the mask of the Hunter, my bow already in my hand. Once I have set my eyes on you it really is just a matter of

Time is my kingdom, just for this night; if I could though, I would stretch it out like soft dough under my fingers, grind your smile into every little grain my hourglasses hold. My Lotus Queen, will you give me this

Dance, dance, this will be like a hunt through the woods, a fugue in the darkness! My fingers feel your heartbeat under them quickening already, my bow string tightens. I release my arrow straight into your heart like a gift, see it hit the center with a vibrato of

Violins were ringing in my ears then, oh Mother! His hand hot against mine one moment then softly pried away by the stranger in the mask of green and crimson. Everybody turned and stared, the dance stopped for just the fraction of a note; people bowed to the crimson masked stranger, cradling my Time King to his chest. But it is just like this for those who dance this ball, the dancers

Change never, my sweet boy. The others, look at them! dance this roundelay for years, from the day their feet can hold the shoes to the day their bones will no longer sing with the melody, hoping all the time to find themselves as lucky as I have made you. You are mine now, and I yours, after a fashion. Come, my sweet boy, let your scarlet silk trickle along my hands like a tongue wet with hunger. Follow me, you will be the King of Time forevermore. Never let anybody tell you that you were not ready to pay the

Price.

Guan Yin in the Garden
Nancy Sheng

Part One: Writing the Shan Hai Jing

I want to touch you where it hurts, he says.
On his fingers there are three things:
crumbling dirt, sorghum wine, and a moth.

They carve her out of wood.
They wrap black silk for her hair.
They put her on their backs and carry her
from their southern village to the Emperor's court,
from the concubines to the mandarins,
from the rice wives to the fruit merchants,
from the saint in the high wharves
to the fish who swim out of the Yellow River.
They lie on their gills and call her name.

All things come from suffering, she says,
and suffering is the beginning of truth.

On her wedding day she pierces her ears with jade,
then goes down the path to meet her husband.

Part Two: Legend of the White Snake

Humans and snakes cannot mate.
She puts her head on his shoulder
and weeps poison that sears him.

Two women sit facing each other.
They have blind eyes and hungry lips.
Between them is a bowl of hexagrams.
Bai says to Xiao Qing,
It's your turn.

Xiao Qing tosses the yarrow.

38: Kui.

Bai kisses her friend on the forehead
and tells her goodbye.

Part Three: The Gate of Metamorphosis

The carp dreams.
The jiang shi walk in towns.

The rain dragon looks up at the sun
and promises eight years of drought.

The boy with the crooked foot
plays his flute to the pigs.
Here little piggies, he sings.
In my belly you'll be warm.

Part Four: The Prince Who Ate Jade

Oh, says his father. Too soft, too soft!
You will never kill enemies this way.
They will overrun the Palace of Respite.
Your mother will be raped,
your brothers put to the sword,
your sisters silenced.
Ai, ai, ai!

His name was Xuan Yuan,
but no one remembered that afterwards.

He puts the comb in his hair
and goes out with a quiver of arrows.
It only takes three shots
for them to call him emperor
and five for them to call him god.

This isn't necessary, he says.
But he is young.
He has time yet for glory.

Part Five: Diaspora

In Chinatown the air smells like anise,
ginger, cassia, cloves, and fennel.
The rubber burns the bilingual signs
while the woman makes her way
through twisted alleys with chicken bone
and looks up to see the third-floor window
shine with the joy of lanterns.

Mama, Baba, she says. It's me.

At first her parents are puzzled.
They stare at this stranger with red lipstick.
With blond highlights, piercings, a short skirt.
But then she ducks her head and smiles
and they kick over the table trying to reach her.

Part Six: Things to Tell Your Children

Guan Yin is the goddess of mercy, she says.

And? he asks.

And what? And nothing. That's it.
You don't need anything more than that.

Ahura Mazda
Michael Shorb

This sand and thistle
wilderness once held
gardens where we greeted
fighting Cambyses home
from Egyptian conquest
with slaves, ivory, gold,
a stable of captured gods.

We feasted; glittering
dancers whirled.
Priests of Ahura Mazda
filled our cups
with liquid glory.

Waking, we found the city under siege.
Macedonian javelins raining down,
runners bawling out the dread
from Granicus. There's a new god now,
Aristotle's prize student,
Alexander Mastodon,
a phalanx of bloody
dust spilling into Asia,
Egypt, India,
like a plague.

Our survey indicates a finite
number of horsehide insect whisks,
Nubian slaves loading bales
of colored cotton,
tusks, spices, pottery,
precious stones and bulging
granaries, newly erected temples.

Then it darkens,
armies roll,

locusts drizzle through
river orchards, illuminated
manuscripts go for fish wrap.

Each human's got a part to play.
I was the grinning wanderer who
played the flute or juggled
green bottles in torchlit courtyards;
I was the plain man with
the shriveled belly,
a bricklayer, a sailmaker,
the man who buried fallen legions
with balm and special markings,
coins lidding the eyes.

This process, profit and loss,
began with dried
fish and **carved elk horn**,
flints and surgery exchanged for
water in summer,
salt in winter.

Fall off a Turkish siege ladder at
Constantinople into a dark vortex
of smoking emptiness
and points
of echoing fire,
see what happens then.

A last memory
will be the full yellow moon,
a woman's touch,
the smile of a friend.

The ideas we know about.
They're always around,
shuffled from fleet to caravan,
maybe getting less attention by now,
being laughed at, ridiculed,
abused in the marketplace.

You simply make less impression
each time you exist.
Begin as a god
deep in the velvet
myths of Persia if you must;
you'll end up propping
open a temple door

in the seedy part of town,
naming a rotary engine
automobile by the time
the 20th century rolls.

An excellent system,
come to think of it.
Natural selection
among archetypes.
Each vehicle becoming its own
model of the universe,
complete with ritualized
accessories,
customized concepts
of duty and freedom.

Me, I love my new
Olympus XL Grand Operatic
camper with dashboard pantheon,
sacred bough orphic stereo tape deck,
barbed-wire doors,
supply of food, fuel, and liquor
ensuring our survival, yours
in the abstract sense,
mine in the concrete sense.

In this vehicle there is nothing to fear.
One recent evening I ploughed through
a mob of irate campesinos
while turning west toward
dusk on the Trans-Amazon Highway.

In my spotlights they scattered,
buzzing and bristling
in the manner
of the starving,
gnashing their teeth
as the weight of my place
in this night—
the only man for miles around
with liquor and food—
dawned on them.

Driving on, I caught a glimpse
of a Roman legion lost in
the Sahara of my rearview mirror
and extinct deer grazing
in a dammed-up canyon.

Now is the perfect time.
My god and I light up a
Cuban cigar, open a bottle of
'46 Bordeaux. The magic radio
comes on with mankind's
greatest hits:
Roland's horn, Oppenheimer's
mushrooming parody of Mozart's
magic flute caress the steaming,
bird-infested darkness.

Now you will hear a music
that does not dream
of what is past or passing
or to come.
Roll up the window
to block out the annoying
vegetable tides.
Listen.

Speaking to the Hangman Is Not Permitted
J. E. Stanley

Eleven jurors:
"Guilty."
One juror:
"Not guilty."

The vote must be unanimous.

The sound of hammering
penetrates the walls,
continues with no break.
Once the scaffold has been completed,
it must be used,
either one time,
or twelve.

We've all seen at least one hanging.
It's the law.
All citizens are required to witness a hanging
before they turn eighteen,
before they can serve on a jury.

I remember too well:
the rope too short to break
the condemned man's neck,

the eternity it took for him to die,
the serene smile on the Hangman's face.

They say that if a jury hangs,
it's different,
quick.
But no one really knows,
since acquittals are all but nonexistent,
and juries are never hanged publicly.
The area is cleared first.

The charges against the defendant,
our defendant:
"On unspecified dates,
said accused did willfully, viciously,
and with malice aforethought
rape and murder an unspecified number
of unidentified women and children.
The prosecution rests."

The defendant protested his innocence,
that he'd never raped or killed anyone,
that there was no evidence presented against him,
no bodies, no witnesses, no dates, nothing,
and no women or children even missing.

Of course, as pointed out by the foreman,
the defendant has a reason to lie,
and he must have done something
for the State to charge him.
Certainly, he must present a danger to Society.

And, besides, we have families.
Lives to return to.
It's all of us or him?
Twelve or one?

The hammering stops
with the one "Not guilty" vote still remaining.

We listen for footsteps,
though we know the Hangman's
approach is always silent.

We jump at each of the two knocks on the door:
the first would be from the bailiff,
standing watch just outside;
the second, from the Hangman himself.

We hear the bailiff's key start to turn.
Eleven pairs of eyes stare only at me.
I look down at my feet
and say,
"Guilty."

**The Legend of the Emperor's Space Suit
(A Tale of Consensus Reality)**
Mary Turzillo

The Emperor of Greater Bluvia,
thinking to impress his favorite concubine,
the exquisite (but innocent) provincial Justina,
bought a ride on EOS, the Earth to Orbit Shuttle.

And to be doubly impressive
(for Emperors can be both egotistical
and insecure),
the Emperor conducted a contest
for the very best space suit design
in which to do his princely space walk,

which Justina would observe
through a powerful telescope
constructed for her and her alone
to observe this majestic EVA

(which stands for Extra Vehicular Activity).

(My darlings, if you disdain
Three-Letter Acronyms,
best read some other legend.)

The space suit engineers
from MIT and RIT and NASA and the ESA
and other acronymic bodies
put out their very best,
constructed of fabrics and plates and flexible joints
almost magical in their resilience,
suits designed to withstand hard vacuum
and cold and heat and even
solar flares and cosmic rays,
also with advanced flexibility and added radios
and onboard bathrooms and showers
and snack tubes and sunlamps
and a fur codpiece in one,
a soothing Thai massage in another,

and flexible motorized motion augmentation
to allow skateboarding
and ballroom dancing
and even hula-hooping.

He rejected each space suit in turn.

Two lowly engineering undergrads
stood at the end of the contest lineup
with nothing, it seemed, but air
between them.
"Do you mock my magnificence?"
roared the Emperor in his most imperious voice.

"No," said the first, a shy
bespectacled sophomore
with a dirty blonde ponytail
and acne scars.
Her partner, who had a way of letting his gaze slide away,
asserted in a squeaky voice,
"Your Magnificence, this suit is designed
with the most advanced optical camouflage
ever developed. Our advisor
holds the patent, but allowed us
to use it, just this once, for your suit.

"Try it. Do, try it."

They helped the Emperor into their suit
and toggled each toggle
and zipped each zipper
and clamped down the helmet
and checked the gauges and hoses
and asked, "How does it feel?"

"It fits like a glove!
Why, I feel as if I am wearing nothing at all!
So light! So transparent!
My hands flex, my knees bend—
You, my children, get the prize."

And his minions wrote the prize check
for three million Euros.

"For hark!" said the undergrads' advisor,
"only the best and brightest understand
and can sense this wonderful space suit.
To the uneducated it will seem invisible."

And the scientists and engineers and astronauts and cosmonauts and taikonauts,
seeing that their own designs had no chance,
began to murmur that it was indeed a fine design;
yes, the lines were a bit blurry,
the color faded into the background,
but that was a good thing,
and they took no exception
to the undergrads' design.

Came the day
when the Emperor arrived
at the Orbiting Star Station,
having overcome
his unseemly space-sickness,
and determined to step through an airlock
into the bright/dark of space
to crown his Imperial feat
as the first Imperial astronaut.

And so he took off all his clothes,
even his majestic jockey shorts
and his Imperial tube socks.

The two undergraduates came forward.
They toggled the toggles
and zipped the zippers
and clamped the helmet
and checked the gauges and hoses
and declared him safe to go
Outside.

And he entered the airlock.
He knew that Justina,
exotic, naive, candid, authentically womanly,
would be watching.
He had commissioned a special telescope
just for her,
and that telescope would be trained on him.
He would wave, and she would wave back.
(Although he wouldn't see her.
One of the losing designs had had a special
video receiver so he could see Justina
at the moment of his triumph,
and for a moment he regretted
not choosing that one,
except it was ugly and clunky
and an unstylish shade of puce,
and the helmet made him look like a popcorn machine.)

He approached the airlock
and the engineers and scientists
and astronauts and cosmonauts and taikonauts
all murmured their admiration
of the brilliant design.

And the Emperor stepped into the air lock,
and the air was voided into space,
and the Emperor showed no discomfort,
for this was a most cunningly designed space suit,
and he gloried in the image he must cut
to his beautiful Justina,
whom he almost married once
except that he couldn't get permission
from his first wife,
whose father ran the biggest bank in Greater Bluvia.

And the Emperor floated to the door of the airlock
and pushed himself out
onto the hull
of the Orbiting Star Station.

The invisible magnetic boots
held him to the metal hull.
The invisible helmet surrounded his head
with the sweetest and most breathable air.
The invisible renewing oxygen tanks
sent deliciously perfumed oxygen
to his Imperial nostrils.

And he said,
This is what it is to be Imperious!
Now I, Emperor of Greater Bluvia,
am truly famous in history as the first
spacefaring Emperor!

And the scientists and engineers
and astronauts and cosmonauts and taikonauts
held their breath, for it was true!
The invisible space suit
was the best space suit ever designed.

And the Emperor began to do jigs and skips
and pirouettes and cartwheels
on the surface of the Orbiting Star Station.
For he was now the greatest,
and his lovely Justina would be impressed
and would love him for himself

and not just for the ten million Euros
he spent on her villa in Lorentz.

And then Justina, trembling with admiration,
set her gaze to the eyepiece of her special telescope.

And she drew back.
For nobody had prepared her.
Nobody had told her what to see.
And she said, "But he is naked!"

She said this on satellite TV.

Now the Emperor,
because he had taken his smartphone with him,
heard this exclamation,
and his skin began to freeze and boil,
and his eyes began to blur,
and his body felt that it might explode,
and the Emperor,
poor Emperor,
very shortly
knew no more.

And the scientists and engineers and astronauts and cosmonauts and taikonauts
and the viewing public and everybody in heaven and earth
saw the Emperor effervesce like a headache tablet in water.

And they said, Yes, I knew it, but I didn't want to say,
and well, the design was innovative, but really—
and I'm glad he was brave enough to be the first to try it.

And this only proves, my darlings,
that the truth is a dangerous thing,
and that neither money nor love nor the acclamation of experts
can save you from hard vacuum.

The Melancholy of Mechagirl
Catherynne M. Valente
(for Dmitri and Jeannine)

X Prefecture drive time radio
    trills and pops
its pink rhinestone bubble tunes—
pipe that sound into my copper-riveted heart,
that softgirl/brightgirl/candygirl electrocheer gigglenoise
right down through the steelfrown tunnels of my

all-hearing head.
     Best stay
out of my way
when I've got my groovewalk going. It's a rhythm
you learn:
move those ironzilla legs
to the cherry-berry vanillacream sparklepop
and your pneumafuel efficiency will increase
according to the Yakihatsu formula (sigma3, 9 to the power of four)

Robots are like Mars: they need
girls.
  Boys won't do;
the memesoup is all wrong. They stomp
when they should kiss
and they're none too keen
on having things shoved inside them.
    You can't convince them
there's nothing kinky going on:
you can't move the machine without IV interface
fourteen intra-optical displays
a codedump wafer like a rose petal
under the tongue,
silver tubes
wrapped around your bones.

  It's just a job.
Why do boys have to make everything
sound weird? It's not a robot
until you put a girl inside. Sometimes
      I feel like that.
      A junkyard
      the Company forgot to put a girl in.

I mean yeah.
My crystal fingers are laser-enabled
light comes out of me
like dawn. Bright orangecream
killpink
sizzling tangerine deathglitter. But what
does it mean? Is this really
a retirement plan?
  All of us Company Girls
sitting in the Company Home
in our giant angular titanium suits
knitting tiny versions of our robot selves
playing poker with xray eyes
crushing the tea kettle with hotlilac chromium fists

every day at 3?

I get a break
every spring.
                Big me
powers down
transparent highly-conductive golden eyeball
by transparent highly-conductive golden eyeball.
                Little me steps out
and the plum blossoms quiver
like a frothy fuchsia baseline.
                My body is
                full of holes
where the junkbody metalgirl tinkid used to be
inside me inside it
and I try to go out for tea and noodles
but they only taste like crystallized cobalt-4
and faithlessness.
I feel my suit
all around me. It wants. I want. Cold scrapcode
                drifts like snow behind my eyes.
I can't understand
why no one sees the dinosaur bones
of my exo-self
dwarfing the ramen-slingers
and their steamscalded cheeks.

                Maybe I go dancing.
                Maybe I light incense.
                Maybe I fuck, maybe I get fucked.
Nothing is as big inside me
as I am
when I am inside me.

                When I am big
I can run so fast
out of my skin
my feet are mighty,
flamecushioned and undeniable.
                I salute with my sadgirl/hardgirl/crunchgirl
purplebolt tungsten hands
the size of cars
                and Saturn tips a ring.

It hurts to be big
but everyone sees me.

                When I am little

when I am just a pretty thing
and they think I am bandaged
to fit the damagedgirl fashionpop manifesto
instead of to hide my nickelplate entrance nodes
        well
I can't get out of that suit either
but it doesn't know how to vibrate
a building under her audioglass palm
until it shatters.

I guess what I mean to say is
I'll never have kids. Chances for promotion
are minimal and my pension
sucks. That's ok.
After all, there is so much work
        to do. Enough for forever.
And I'm so good at it.
All my sitreps shine
like so many platinum dolls.
I'm due for a morphomod soon—
I'll be able to double over at the waist
like I've had something cut out of me
and fold up into a magentanosed Centauri-capable spaceship.
        So I've got that going for me.
At least fatigue isn't a factor. I have a steady
decalescent greengolden stream
of sourshimmer stimulants
available at the balling of my toes.
        On balance, to pay for the rest
    well
you've never felt anything
like a pearlypink ball of plasmid clingflame
releasing from your mouth
like a burst of song.
        And Y Prefecture
is just so close by.

The girls and I talk.
    We say:
start a dream journal.
take up ikebana.
make your own jam.
    We say:
Next spring
let's go to Australia together
look at the kangaroos.
    We say:
turn up that sweet vibevox happygirl music

tap the communal PA
we've got a long walk ahead of us today
and at the end of it
a fire like six perfect flowers
arranged in an iron vase.

The Secret of Being a Cowboy
Catherynne M. Valente

Did I ever tell you I used to be a cowboy?
       It's true.
Had a horse name of Drunk Bob
a six shooter
called Witty Rejoinder.
       And I tell you what,
       Me and Bob and Witty
       we rode the fucking range.

This thing here is two poems and one's about proper shit
mythic, I guess, just the way you like it and the other one
isn't much to look at, mostly about what a horse smells like
when he's been slurping up Jack and ice from the trough.

The first poem goes like this:

A few little-known facts about cowboys:

       Most of us are girls.
       Obsolescence does not trouble us.
       We have a dental plan.

What I can tell you is cows smell like office work and
the moon looks like Friday night and the paycheck just cashed
rolling down to earth like all the coins
I ever earned.

Drunk Bob he used to say to me:
son, carrying you's no hurt—
it's your shadow weighs me down.

That, and your damned singing.

And Witty she'd chuckle
like the good old girl she was,
with a cheeky spin of her barrel
she'd whistle:

boy, just gimme a chance
I'll knock your whole world down.

Me and Bob and Witty,
we rode town to town and sometimes we had cattle
and sometimes we didn't and that's just how it lies.
Full-time cowboy employment is a lot like being a poet.
It's a lot of time spent on your lonesome in the dark
and most folks don't rightly know
what it is you do
but they're sure as shot they could manage it
just about as well as you.

Some number of sweethearts come standard with the gig,
though never too much dough.
They dig the clothes, but they can't shoot for shit,
and they damn sure don't want to hear your poems.
That's all right.
I got a heart like a half bottle
of no-label whiskey.
Nothing to brag on,
but enough for you, and all your friends, too.

I quit the life
for the East Coast and a novel I never could finish.
A book's like a cattle drive—you pound back and forth over the same
ugly patch of country until you can taste your life seeping out
like tin leeching into the beans
but it's never really over.

Drunk Bob said:
kid, you were the worst ride I had
since Pluto said: Bob, we oughta get ourselves a girl.

And Witty whispers: *six, baby, count them up* and just like that
we're in the other poem, which is how we roll
on the glory-humping, dust-gulping, ever-loving range.
Some days you can't even get a man to spit in your beer
and some you crack open your silver gun
and there's seeds there like blood already freezing
ready to stand tall at high midnight
ready to fire so fucking loyal, so sweet,
like every girl who ever said no
turning around at once and opening their arms.

And your honor's out on the table, all cards hid.
And by your honor I mean my honor,
and by my honor I mean everything in me, always, forever,

everything in a body that knows
what to do with six ruby bullets
and a horse the color of two in the morning.

That knows when the West tastes like death and an old paperback
you saddle your shit and ride East,
when you're done with it all you don't put down roots
and Drunk Bob says: *come on, son, you've got that book to write
and I know a desk in the dark with your name on it.*
And Witty old girl she sighs: *you know what you have to do.
Seeds fire and bullets grow and I'm the only one who's ever loved you.
That horse can go hang.*
And I say: maybe I'll get an MFA
and be King of the Underworld
in some sleepy Massachusetts town.

And all the while my honor's tossed into the pot
and by my honor I mean your honor
or else what's this all about? Drunk Bob
never did know where this thing was going
but I guess the meat of it is how Bob is strong and I am strong
and Witty is a barrel of futures, and we are all of us
unstopping, unending, unbeginning:
we keep moving. You gotta keep moving.
Six red bullets will show the way down.

    We all have to bring the cows in.

I am here to tell you
we are all of us just as mighty as planets—and you too,
we'll let you in, we've got stalwart to spare—
but you might have to sleep on the floor.
    Me and Bob and Witty just
clop on and the gun don't soften
and the horse don't bother me with questions,
all of us just heading toward the red rhyme of the sunset
and the door at the bottom of the verse.

The secret of being a cowboy is
never sticking around too long and honor
sometimes looks like a rack of bones
still standing straight up at the end of both poems.

Blood, Snow, Birch and Underworld
JoSelle Vanderhooft

I.
A daughter like a window:
full as glass
and just as empty.
The queen sucked her forefinger—the one
ever responsible for accidents,
and thought a canyon in her forehead.

Girls like blood and winter and bare branches.
All the rage, like hearts in strong boxes,
dolls in see-through coffins,
little dogs in little bags.
But what is popular is deadly as starvation,
and just as catching.

A mother knows this,
when her own did not. Knows
the terror of monstrosity in miniature.

Three red drops on white,
the shellacked sill a perfect frame.
The glass between flawless,
Invisible.
Correct.

The finger circumnavigates her navel,
dips into its wishing well.
Such a daughter: beautiless as air,
No heart
and no guts.
Invisible
and safe.

Her own gut moved,
complicit.

II.
Cardinal on birch.
Snow between.

Ballet-balanced Cipher watches him
tilt head, shake wing—
twitch like the physick's organs
electrified for the king's curiosity.

"It's like this, majesty—"
a flipped switch,
the heart's veins hop.
"The blood travels on a circuit,
like the seasons."

The Court applauded.
Unnoticed,
she closed her hand over her breast,
thought of living fruit.
Her own heart, certainly,
did no such thing.

The cardinal perks,
vanishes into December.
She watches, strokes her breast
again.

It doesn't beat.
Not even when Mother died.

Not even when Father dismissed the doctor,
called for something
softer, more attractive.

It makes no noise at all.
Not even my footsteps do.

Sometimes,
sometimes
she thinks everyone
knows her emptiness,
looks through her like this windowpane
in search
of something red.

III.
Stepmother
is Mother's reverse.

Skin like grave-loam,
hair curled
brown
as wasting ivy,
dry and thin-ribbed winter
for her predecessor's hips and bounty,
for her pallor less snowfall than August sun.

Even the mouth is different:
Knife-gash, menses smear—
Obscene, titters the Court.
Not button-prim like their Lady
who ate only in nibbles
and touched no wine.

Cipher does not think it so.
It is the first that smiles.
"You're Cipher, right?"
Not daughter, princess,
window.
Her lips draw into a seed. "Well,
my dear?
Don't be afraid."

Her smile
is the winter sun
between drives of schorl clouds.

A cardinal's wing shadows the clerestory;
Cipher's fingers flutter to her breasts.
Beneath her touch, a twist in hollowness.

Something is not there
that wants to be.

Stepmother's tongue
tastes the corner of her lips.
"Interesting."

IV.
The year's wheel turns from snow
to colder snow.
Midwinter visits in her holly wreathes,
and crowns of candle fire.
It is a holiday, Stepmother says,
so let the balustrades wear evergreen;
the tables and ladies
moan with seedcakes and sweetmeats.
Her eyes reflect the hearth, amber
upon amber.
Cipher swirls a sugar cube, considers—the stars
of Tartarus must look the same.
At her left hand, Stepmother laughs a toast;
the stars turn to her
     and burn.
Stepmother smiles a wealth of fire opal,

leans in for a secret—
"The birch when everyone's abed."—
clinks stein with Ladies and then Father,
choreography subtler than wind.

Cipher's breath snags in her ribs—
the new sun ascends between her legs.

V.
The moon is full when dreams of emerald
and amber fall off like a sheet.
The air bites Cipher's breasts beneath her gown.
The flagstones nip her heels,
snow bites her toes.

The sky's unraveling quartz,
lapis, chalcedony. Snowflake
obsidian catches upon her lashes,
veils everything in air
and the moonstone winter-light of—

Stepmother
at the birch,
hair a wave of darkness,
smile like the sickle moon.
Empty calls to
Empty.
She waves benediction—
beckon: Come.
steps through the hanging trees.
Her gown is a tear of ruby
cardinal wing.

Cipher follows,
does not blink away the snow
that settles in her eyes.

Stepmother's burning,
beacon through elder, oak
yew and prickle-pine.
Trees stranger, tall
and ragged. Twigs of diamond,
drusy, chrysocolla pull her skirts,
brush back her bangs,
won't wait—Stepmother
moves like corpse candle light,
in mist direction,
but purposeful as plagues.

The darkness parts
upon another red—
tree bare as black pearl
spread ventrical

Fruit beating
each
a heart.

Stepmother
shifts like circulation,
cups one pomegranate,
brings it to her hands.
"Do you know
how you were planted?"

The wind whispers
in shades
In cautions.
Cipher does not listen,
hears only the beat
of living seeds.

She shakes her head, embarrassed.

Stepmother smiles,
like gold might smile.
"Carefully," she says,
"like harvest grain,
like potash in fire:
for another's purpose."
"Tell me,"—
the pomegranate cradled in her hand—
"what need has either
soil or window
for a heart?"

The wind ripples their hair like sails
and there is a space beneath her ribs.
Cipher feels above it,
reaches—

"Hurt is in the taking."
Stepmother strokes the red curve.
"Eat, and there will be hunger,
want, rejection.
Death, too—
For seeds must die to yield.

Eat not,
You will know the story of a window—
empty
as the world is full."

The fruit is ice inside her palm,
heavy, cold—
familiar as the space
—that must be filled.
Cipher shuts her eyes
and plucks.

The seeds stick like stars
inside her.

VI.
Stepmother vanishes
like hoarfrost.
The palace forgets her like a dream.

The cardinal hops branch,
shakes snow from wings like waking.
Cipher smiles
like a window opened,
and a breath

    Escaped.

Initiation
Caitlin Meredith Walsh

You must go alone.
Wait until the light
has turned red and begun to die.
If you go in the daylight,
either you will be caught, or
you will not find anything.

You must find a tunnel
underneath the city street.
I cannot tell you where,
or which one;
you will know it when you see it.
It will be
dark, low-ceilinged,
its walls made of stone.
This will not be easy;

there may be more than one.
The one you want will have
pictures painted on its stones
by the ones who came before you.
Some of these will be very old.
Some will have faded,
become pale and weathered
with time.

There will be one brick,
one stone
that is loose.
Pull it free; it is the right one.

Look into the space behind it,
the gap, the empty hole
in the wall or the roof.
At first you will see
darkness, only darkness.
Keep trying;
you are not looking hard enough.

Then
you may see it,
or you may not:
a light, or many lights,
a pinwheel made of tiny chips
of glass, of ice, of heat.
A galaxy, if you like,
a perfect galaxy you could carry in your pocket,
preserve under clear glass
or crush with one hand, if you chose.
A whole galaxy, hidden in a tunnel
under the dirty street.

It will change you, this thing.
I cannot say how;
it is different for everyone.
You will not know how you have changed
until much later.

After you have seen it,
put the stone back
and leave a picture, any picture, on the wall
to join the others,
to show that you were there.
Then leave this place
and do not come back again.

Should you want to come back,
you will find no tunnel like the one you remember,
no pictures on the stone.
Some places you may visit only once;
there is no going back.

The Soldier's Return
Kyla Lee Ward

The ride was hard and howling dark
had bitten me through to the bone,
but how could I begrudge its mark
now every hillock spoke of home?

When lanterns scattered like bright seed
across black fields inscribed a sign—
the only writ I cared to read!
Oh what a welcome would be mine!

Returning I to kith and kin
with honor and a soldier's pay
and tales of valor, to begin
the life I might have thrown away.

Returning I a broidered scarf
so softly laid across my hands
by one whose sorrow still could laugh
with eyes that haunted other lands.

And as the moon surpassed the cloud,
shedding a pale and pure light,
I thought how sweetly she had vowed
to wait and watch for me by night.

I led my jennet through the slick
and sighing shade within the trees.
I felt the brush and scatter quick
of things unseen about my knees.

I seemed enspelled to make no sound:
I'm not one to imagine bane,
but now I felt unease confound
my joy as smoke the moon might stain.

So to a secret, sheltered dell,
of frosted grass and blackened fern,
that in our childhood we knew well,

and once of age we did not spurn.

Then from the black rose silver-white:
my love, my love was standing there,
and though she looked as angel might,
I saw the vervain in her hair.

On Sunday mornings, piously,
I'd seen her kneel before the cross,
had heard her praised for modesty
and tending well her father's house.

Had kissed her lips and held her near,
but never gone beyond those bounds.
How could it be that I saw here
the signs that sorcery surrounds?

The dagger and the smoking brands,
the cockerel with broken crest,
the bloody basin in her hands,
the star encircled on her breast.

The wind shook both the low and tall,
as though the sky had royal tides
and here came madness, drowning all
my horror and my fear besides!

There could be thunder passing through,
or did I hear the martial drum
I left behind? All that I knew
was if she beckoned, I must come.

But on the blood her gaze was set,
a dreadful working to begin,
and as the fumes did twist and fret
I vow I saw myself within.

My image rode amidst the haze
of flame consuming croft and town;
I saw me set the rooves ablaze
and cut the fleeing people down.

I saw me seize the sacral gold,
a fearful priest wasting his breath.
The boy whose cowardice I told,
making him seek a needless death.

The children whose last crust I seized,

and other gallant deeds I did;
the men I'd slaughtered on their knees,
the women I had roughly rid.

I saw her see all that I was
and thought that I could leave behind.
No matter whose the crown or cause,
here I would no redemption find.

And did she pass? For she was gone,
perhaps into the tinctured air,
perhaps in shape of foal or fawn
that passed and left me standing there.

And so, my love, we wander yet,
each with our secret to repine.
How can we our course homeward set
now I know yours and you know mine?

All Souls' Day
Shannon Connor Winward

The tree has lost her colors early
but she remembers me
she murmurs under my hands
and opens her arms wide

I crawl into her lap
I whisper my name
I pull my sweater tighter
against November's sky

Her bony branches snare
a canopy of mists
if the veils can ever part
it would be now

and here, where the ground
holds my stones,
my stories
like little unmarked graves

It takes a certain alchemy
an arrangement of bones
crisscross in a cradle of wood
bark, soil, flesh, and stone

If I close my eyes, I can feel them
drawn like spirits to light
a fairy ring of once-was girls
a circle of the ghosts of me

One in pigtails
one with scars
one who bangs her fists
upon the bark

She gathers blossoms
she gathers wishes
she weaves resentments
like a crown

She wields twigs like swords
she reads sheltered from the sun
she wraps her pain in snakeskin
and buries it among the roots

I hear her singing, praying
I know her thoughts
I live again her promise
to leave the past behind

but I know what she is
too young to understand
all selves are fleeting
and tomorrow never comes

Each day I have to bury
the one who came before me
each night I make way for
another self yet to be born

She won't be the one to
overcome it. She is long gone
but if ever the way to her is
open, it would be *this*.

It takes a certain frame of mind
memories gathered, a joining of hands
on the day of all souls, briefly
we are whole again.

Ribbons of the Sun
Greer Woodward

In a summer garden
Long ago,
I saw a sylphid dancing.
She was young and wild,
A windborne child,
Barefoot and entrancing.
She took my hand and
Twirled me round and round;
Our feet made perfect
Music on the ground;
And when our magic dance
Was finally done,
She gave me golden
Ribbons of the sun.

In a fragrant garden
Long ago,
The sylphid danced for hours.
With a scarlet rose
Between her toes,
She wafted through the flowers.
She showed me how to
Gambol with the breeze,
To pirouette beside
The peonies;
And when our silent
Shadows moved as one,
She vanished like a
Ribbon of the sun.

And somehow
I could see
A thousand dances
Meant for me;
Whirling round
A willow tree,
I glimpsed the
Zephyr dancer
I could be.

In a crowded city
Far from home,
I am a dancer striving,

Working week by week
On my technique,
And my day is arriving.
I dance to free a
Cadence of the heart,
The sure steps of my
Sylphid counterpart;
And when my feet and
Feelings move as one,
I'm holding golden
Ribbons of the sun.

Mood of Mind (I)—*Tu Bi Hi Xa*
Xanadu (Ofnguyenfame)

Far from believers towards
the end of the temple
four pairs of pillars' distance
He shines in golden-reddish
like a perfect sunset
(rise when you like!)

    Dress as matter as Earth—

As earthy His dress
as spiritual His skin
shining like Sun's Son
though sticking to vicious gravity
head turning up from
base and naked neck
like Inti from
surrounding halves
foldings in neck just past
of many shades
that draw features
like moon at night
still glancing in
Princess and Daoist monk
who was supposed to return
her from exile

Struck as by vertical
lightning from atop
He may look a little
older than He is—
like images of Mama Quilla
delay His age by, say, a quarter—

just left behind Him
a fluorescent radiating &
rotating cycle of green, red, and yellow
as radiant as one could expect
His forehead chakra to beat time
on closer inspection
when one focuses attention
to His face that far
a way to Enlightenment

One may try and discern
color of His headdress
that likes purple more than yellow
though through an interface of brown—
so it seems—and from all settings it is obvious
that His experience can only beat appearance
and that experience is more lively than one may guess
and after and before all it's Whom we are—

His eyes seem open wide
His cheeks long and square
His mouth caught in an
indefinable shade reflection
which does not reveal any

> *Mood of Mind*—

whether it's laughing or serene
rainy, sunny, or cloudy
when lips are thin and broad
horizontal emphasized
by wrinkles to His neck
not yet betraying any
advancing age, worries, or fatigue
but imperfections of body
being linked to mind

Longevity large earlobes remind us
again we are looking
at Buddha as it may sign
a supernatural feature
though it is naturally possible
though less probable nowadays
and bring a halt to hours of
anthropomorphic reflection
though it's all that religion could beat—
both listening silence and enjoying

rejoicing on a holiday
like Tet 2 to 2day
(rice's free if you feel so!)

Xanadu (Ofnguyenfame) for the Rhysling Awards (May 2012): Thanks to Ambassador's Pagoda Hanoi Tracy Chapman and UNESCO. "Mood of Mind" is part of In Search of Buddhas' Smile, *www.angelfire.com/blog/xanaduarts/in_search_of_buddhas_smile/*

THE RHYSLING AWARD WINNERS: 1978-2011

1978	Long	Gene Wolfe	"The Computer Iterates the Greater Trumps"
	Short	Duane Ackerson	"The Starman"
	(tie)	Sonya Dorman	"Corruption of Metals"
		Andrew Joron	"Asleep in the Arms of Mother Night"
1979	Long	Michael Bishop	"For the Lady of a Physicist"
	Short	Duane Ackerson	"Fatalities"
	(tie)	Steve Eng	"Storybooks and Treasure Maps"
1980	Long	Andrew Joron	"The Sonic Flowerfall of Primes"
	Short	Robert Frazier	"Encased in the Amber of Eternity"
	(tie)	Peter Payack	"The Migration of Darkness"
1981	Long	Thomas M. Disch	"On Science Fiction"
	Short	Ken Duffin	"Meeting Place"
1982	Long	Ursula K. Le Guin	"The Well of Baln"
	Short	Raymond DiZazzo	"On the Speed of Sight"
1983	Long	Adam Cornford	"Your Time and You: A Neoprole's Dating Guide"
	Short	Alan P. Lightman	"In Computers"
1984	Long	Joe Haldeman	"Saul's Death: Two Sestinas"
	Short	Helen Ehrlich	"Two Sonnets"
1985	Long	Siv Cedering	"Letter from Caroline Herschel (1750–1848)"
	Short	Bruce Boston	"For Spacers Snarled in the Hair of Comets"
1986	Long	Andrew Joron	"Shipwrecked on Destiny Five"
	Short	Susan Palwick	"The Neighbor's Wife"
1987	Long	W. Gregory Stewart	"Daedalus"
	Short	Jonathan V. Post	"Before the Big Bang: News from the Hubble Large Space Telescope"
	(tie)	John Calvin Rezmerski	"A Dream of Heredity"
1988	Long	Lucius Shepard	"White Trains"
	Short	Bruce Boston	"The Nightmare Collector"
	(tie)	Suzette Haden Elgin	"Rocky Road to Hoe"
1989	Long	Bruce Boston	"In the Darkened Hours"
	(tie)	John M. Ford	"Winter Solstice, Camelot Station"
	Short	Robert Frazier	"Salinity"
1990	Long	Patrick McKinnon	"dear spacemen"
	Short	G. Sutton Breiding	"Epitaph for Dreams"

Year	Category	Author	Title
1991	Long	David Memmott	"The Aging Cryonicist in the Arms of His Mistress Contemplates the Survival of the Species While the Phoenix Is Consumed by Fire"
	Short	Joe Haldeman	"Eighteen Years Old, October Eleventh"
1992	Long	W. Gregory Stewart	"the button and what you know"
	Short	David Lunde	"Song of the Martian Cricket"
1993	Long	William J. Daciuk	"To Be from Earth"
	Short	Jane Yolen	"Will"
1994	Long	W. Gregory Stewart and Robert Frazier	"Basement Flats: Redefining the Burgess Shale"
	Short (tie)	Bruce Boston	"Spacer's Compass"
		Jeff VanderMeer	"Flight Is for Those Who Have Not Yet Crossed Over"
1995	Long	David Lunde	"Pilot, Pilot"
	Short	Dan Raphael	"Skin of Glass"
1996	Long	Margaret B. Simon	"Variants of the Obsolete"
	Short	Bruce Boston	"Future Present: A Lesson in Expectation"
1997	Long	Terry A. Garey	"Spotting UFOs While Canning Tomatoes"
	Short	W. Gregory Stewart	"Day Omega"
1998	Long	Laurel Winter	"why goldfish shouldn't use power tools"
	Short	John Grey	"Explaining Frankenstein to His Mother"
1999	Long	Bruce Boston	"Confessions of a Body Thief"
	Short	Laurel Winter	"egg horror poem"
2000	Long	Geoffrey A. Landis	"Christmas (after we all get time machines)"
	Short	Rebecca Marjesdatter	"Grimoire"
2001	Long	Joe Haldeman	"January Fires"
	Short	Bruce Boston	"My Wife Returns as She Would Have It"
2002	Long	Lawrence Schimel	"How to Make a Human"
	Short	William John Watkins	"We Die as Angels"
2003	Long	Charles Saplak and Mike Allen	"Epochs in Exile: A Fantasy Trilogy"
	(tie)	Sonya Taaffe	"Matlacihuatl's Gift"
	Short	Ruth Berman	"Potherb Gardening"
2004	Long	Theodora Goss	"Octavia Is Lost in the Hall of Masks"
	Short	Roger Dutcher	"Just Distance"

2005	Long	Tim Pratt	"Soul Searching"
	Short	Greg Beatty	"No Ruined Lunar City"
2006	Long	Kendall Evans and David C. Kopaska-Merkel	"The Tin Men"
	Short	Mike Allen	"The Strip Search"
2007	Long	Mike Allen	"The Journey to Kailash"
	Short	Rich Ristow	"The Graven Idol's Godheart"
2008	Long	Catherynne M. Valente	"The Seven Devils of Central California"
	Short	F. J. Bergmann	"Eating Light"
2009	Long	Geoffrey A. Landis	"Search"
	Short	Amal El-Mohtar	"Song for an Ancient City"
2010	Long	Kendall Evans and Samantha Henderson	"In the Astronaut Asylum"
	Short	Ann K. Schwader	"To Theia"
2011	Long	C. S. E. Cooney	"The Sea King's Second Bride"
	Short	Amal El-Mohtar	"Peach-Creamed Honey"

SFPA GRAND MASTER AWARD WINNERS

1999	Bruce Boston
2005	Robert Frazier
2008	Ray Bradbury
2010	Jane Yolen

For a complete list of Rhysling winners, runners-up, and nominees, see the Science Fiction Poetry Association archive at http://sfpoetry.com/ra/rhysarchive.html.

HOW TO JOIN THE SFPA

Our members receive four issues of *Star*Line: The Journal of the Science Fiction Poetry Association*, filled with poetry, reviews, articles, and more. Members also receive a copy of the annual Rhysling anthology, containing the best SF/F/H poetry of the previous year (selected by the membership), and *Dwarf Stars*, an edited anthology of the best short-short speculative poetry of the previous year. Each member is allowed to nominate one short poem and one long poem to be printed in the Rhysling anthology and then vote for which poems should receive the Rhysling Award. Members nominate minimalist poetry to the *Dwarf Stars* editor and vote for that award as well.

SFPA Membership — One Year
$15 • PDF only for *Star*Line, Dwarf Stars, Rhysling Anthology*
$30.00 • United States
$35.00 • Canada/Mexico
$40.00 • Overseas

Ten Years
Payable in two equal payments over a period of two years (20 percent savings).
$120 • PDF only
$240 • United States
$280 • Canada/Mexico
$320 • Overseas
Failure to make each payment reverts your membership to the number of years equivalent to the amount actually paid.

Lifetime
Payable in three payments over a period of three years.
$200 • PDF only
$450 • United States
$500 • Canada/Mexico
$550 • Overseas
Failure to make each payment reverts your membership to the number of years equivalent to the amount actually paid.

All prices are in U.S. funds. Checks and money orders should be made out to the Science Fiction Poetry Association and sent to:
    Deborah Flores
    SFPA Treasurer
    P.O. Box 4846
    Covina, CA 91723
    SFPATreasurer@gmail.com
Online and credit card payments should be sent via PayPal to SFPATreasurer@gmail.com.

www.ingramcontent.com/pod-product-compliance
Lightning Source LLC
Chambersburg PA
CBHW032357040426
42451CB00006B/46